ATHEISM

IS VOLUME

91

OF THE

Twentieth Century Encyclopedia of Catholicism

UNDER SECTION

IX

THE CHURCH AND THE MODERN WORLD

IT IS ALSO THE

69TH

VOLUME IN ORDER OF PUBLICATION

THE TWENTIETH CENTURY ENCYCLOPEDIA OF CATHOLICISM

Edited by HENRI DANIEL-ROPS of the Académie Française

ATHEISM

By *ÉTIENNE BORNE*

Translated from the French by S. J. TESTER

HAWTHORN BOOKS · PUBLISHERS · *New York*

First Edition, July, 1961

CONTENTS

INTRODUCTION: THE PROBLEM

THE TRUE FACE OF ATHEISM

Atheism is clearly always a possible view for man in a world in which God is not immediately evident. No age before modern times, however, and in these times no man more than Nietzsche, has had such a vivid awareness of its nature and meaning. So, to conjure up the true face of atheism and take a synoptic view of it in all its might and power, we need only recall Nietzsche's great imprecations. There is in these famous words no doubtful twilight but the full blaze of the noonday sun:

> "Where is God gone?" he called out. "I mean to tell you! *We have killed him*,—you and I! We are all his murderers! But how have we done it? How were we able to drink up the sea?... Whither do we move?... Do we not stray as through infinite nothingness?... God is dead! God remains dead! And we have killed him! How shall we console ourselves, the most murderous of all murderers?... Is not the magnitude of this deed too great for us? Shall we not ourselves have to become Gods, merely to seem worthy of it? There never was a greater event,—and on account of it, all who are born after us belong to a higher history than any history hitherto!"[1]

These fulminations show clearly enough that atheism is diametrically opposed to a mournful unbelief or to a despairing agnosticism, which condemn man to an eternal doubt on

---

[1] Nietzsche, *The Joyful Wisdom* (*La Gaya Scienza*), III, p. 125; trans. T. Common, in vol. 10 of authorized English translation, ed. O. Levy, London, Allen and Unwin, and New York, Macmillan, 1910.

fundamental questions. Atheism, the deliberate, definite, dogmatic denial of the existence of God, and specifically of the God
of the religious consciousness, is not satisfied with approximate
or relative truth, but claims to see the ins and outs of the
game quite clearly: being the absolute denial of the Absolute,
atheism must make itself safe from the attacks of doubt.
God is dead, to use Nietzsche's words, for he is a human
invention, and shares the precariousness which is the lot of all
that is "human, all too human". Transcendence and mystery
are dismissed as mistakes, distorted ideas produced by the
imagination, which in man's earliest history made a fantastic
and illusory world.

True atheism, therefore, will not allow itself to be treated as a
speculative, hypothetical system, entering the lists in the field
of ideas alongside other systems, for more—and more properly
—than any philosophy it thinks of itself as a heroic action, a
historical event. For man had created a sublime dream, which
he cherished more than his very self; the force of inertia and the
comfortableness of inveterate habit would have preserved this
tyranny indefinitely, with its hypocritical consolation which
shielded men from the harshness of reality and from the terrible
beauty of the world. So God could not die a natural death. In
order that the world, for so long darkened by this vast Shadow,
might at last emerge into the light, man had to take upon himself the impossible crime, to murder God, and, as himself the
only creator, cast back into nothingness the monstrous delusion
he had made, which had so crushed his long childhood and
adolescence. Modern atheism is thus not simply an intellectual
negation: it is—and shares with Nietzsche the proud boast—
the crime of all crimes, the heroism above all heroism, in
which the thought is bound up with the action, the murder
of God.

Hence modern atheism is animated by a kind of prophetic
inspiration. This too can be found in Nietzsche. At the an-
nouncement of the death of God, man's prehistory is finished
with and there begins the only history worthy of the name, the

history of man delivered at a blow from all mythology and all superstition, at last capable of creating his own destiny and attaining to his true nature as man. Contemporary Communism, the rationalism and collectivism of which so radically contradict the romanticism and individualism of Zarathustra, is yet an amazingly literal realization of Nietzsche's prophecies. Through Communism, an atheist creed, Marxism, is the creating and animating principle of a totalitarian social system, a system which from Prague to Peking, right across the greatest continental land mass on the globe, submerges half of Europe and half of Asia without allowing any internal opposition. Modern atheism is a mass phenomenon, and its stern intolerance means to rule over the whole future of mankind.

More than ever, then, atheism and religious consciousness are opposed one to the other as the limits of negation and affirmation, so that war between them is inevitable, all possibility of compromise, toleration or reconciliation being completely removed. Between the "God is dead" of the atheist and the "God is living" of the believer, what middle term can there be? The religious consciousness, and particularly that Christian consciousness which modern atheism has seen as the enemy to be attacked and destroyed, is faced with its ultimate trial, which it must bear and overcome: a trial of strength from which will result the total victory of the one and the total defeat of the other, and a trial of strength of mind also in a duel of intellects. Whichever comprehends the other is the conqueror, for to comprehend is to enfold, to dissolve, to pass beyond. Our task in this short book is simply to describe modern atheism as carefully as we can, and to show at the same time that Christianity is not incapable of comprehending atheism nor of understanding, better than it has been able to understand itself, this solitary voice which in the nineteenth century thought it was announcing the death of God and, in the twentieth, in the form in which despite itself it has been realized in history, strives to be a cultural and political creed for the masses. A truth as fundamental and ultimate as that of the existence of

God can be known by this, that whoever contradicts it confirms it without knowing that he does so.

ATHEISM AND ITS FORMS

This preliminary sketch is an endeavour to indicate in a few lines a picture of atheism as it is in essentials; a misleading picture, since in actual fact things are more confused and obscure that it would lead one to think. The word "atheism" has a number of different meanings which cannot all be reduced to one and the same basic signification.

What may be called practical atheism must be left aside. Practical atheism is not the denial of the existence of God, but complete godlessness of action; it is a moral evil, implying not the denial of the absolute validity of the moral law but simply rebellion against that law. Believers conforming to a dead faith and to Pharisaic habits of worship may be practical atheists, though they may attack atheism with high-sounding eloquence. The practical atheism of too many Christians certainly encourages religious indifference and unbelief, but it would be wrong to make of it the sole source of the atheism of the godless.

Properly speaking, the essence of atheism—the *alpha privativum* is proof—is a negation. Now a negation only takes its meaning from the idea it opposes. So there could be as many forms of atheism as there are ideas of God to be attacked or denied. The rejection or denial of God's existence may thus be ambiguous, for the true God may be misunderstood and misconceived by a debased religion that falls to the level of superstition; the idea of God is then changed into an idol, and a religion that is self-contained, self-contented, self-preserving, will defend its false god not only against the wanton denial of the rebel against all authority but also against the denial of the iconoclast who, inspired by a purer religion, shatters its clumsy images of the divine. Victims of a confusion common in the history of religious persecutions, the sophist and the prophet of truth often fall under the same accusation of atheism. There are cases, such as that of Socrates, in which wickedness is added to misunderstanding in the charge of impiety or atheism. What is called atheism can thus cover the worst and lowest or the highest and best: the violent eradication of all wisdom, an undertaking of pride or despair, or a heroic effort, inspired by the Spirit, to resist the lapses into the flesh of the religious mind. So it happens that the distinction between these two kinds of atheism may not be easy and is sometimes impossible to draw, for the most offensively destructive atheism can also, partially and accidentally, help to raise the religious mind towards the infinite and the absolute.

Even when atheism is really atheist, rejecting all transcendence and mystery, it cannot escape another most serious and most significant ambiguity. When it replaces what it destroys, substituting for the God of the traditional religious consciousness some absolute which is rationally knowable, such as the Humanity of the positivists or the History of the Marxists, is it still truly atheism? To use the terms generally employed, does it not become pantheism when it passes in this way from denial to affirmation? This God who has no mystery and is completely accessible to man performs in his immanence the functions of the God of religion for, to take the highest examples, he explains and justifies what is, distinguishes good from evil, condemns and absolves without appeal. Atheism thus becomes its own opposite, but the denial of the true God is thereby only the more radical.

Truly atheist atheism must surely be rather that which sets nothing above or beyond the "No", but makes the only absolute, and the supreme act of the spirit, the denial of any absolute, transcendent or immanent. When—to use Nietzsche's way of speaking—men have become gods by the death of God, is God's kingdom really replaced by the kingdom of man? Or is it rather true, as is hinted in the despair felt behind the passionate sincerity of Nietzsche, that the very idea of an ordered kingdom, divine or human, is shattered, so that man is

abandoned to the chances of "a tale told by an idiot . . . signi-
fying nothing"? Perhaps this kind of pure atheism will show
itself to be more stoutly opposed, theoretically as well as practically, to the God of those hypostasized powers than to the
God of the Gospel and the Sermon on the Mount. Here again
the distinction, even when clearly established, between forms of
atheism opposed to one another is only ideal and is not free
from ambiguity, so much are its forms confused with one
another. Atheism is an equivocal word: sharp but like a two-
edged sword, a mixture of thought and emotion, ambiguous in
its very style. The question is, do these ambiguities reveal an
instability and a contradiction at the very heart of atheism? Is
it not the fate of atheism to split into two contradictory forms,
each inconsistent with the other, each necessary to the other?
An atheist thought, an atheist life, ideally worked out and
lived within, are their own refutation. We must, then, accept
the risk of "sympathizing" (in the etymological sense of sharing
suffering) with atheism in order both to understand and to
destroy it.

PLAN OF PROCEDURE

It remains to be shown that such a suggestion can be justified
and does not sin by presumption. We have only anticipated the
road ahead in order to get from this rough outline, which is
certainly over-hasty and premature, an idea of our plan of
procedure: for a method is always a consequence of certain
preformed ideas.

Since the purpose of the present essay is to make a critical
assessment of contemporary atheism, the first question that
must be raised concerns its origins and originality. From Marx
to Sartre, atheism can be shown to derive, even if—indeed,
especially if—atheists loudly deny it, from Hegel's philosophy;
more exactly, from a particular point in that philosophy.
Atheist polemics against transcendence have for half a century
owed almost everything to Hegel's famous argument against

the "unhappy consciousness". Even in all its diversity of opposing forms, contemporary atheism all goes back to the same basic, initial step, which may not be peculiarly modern: that which seeks in the death of God the advent, the liberation, of man, who thus becomes, in the well-known phrase, his own Prometheus. The image is an ancient one; the ideal also may seem rather older than modern times. Analysis may be able to make clearer the generating principle of atheism and see it under the triple aspect of a permanent possibility of the spirit, a modern venture and an ancient memory, pre-Christian and perhaps pre-Socratic. This is the first question to be tackled.

Having reduced atheism to its basic unity, we shall pass from the singular to the plural, from its essential nature to its various conflicting manifestations. Lyrical and prophetic in Nietzsche, it sinks in Marxism into a heavy materialist and positivist prose. When Sartre carries atheism to the point of a provocative cynicism, this is less from any failing of his ethics than from an excess of logic. What is called "atheist existentialism" can, however, attain in Camus, for example, to a greater nobility and to an ethic as it were stripped to its essence; but this solitary thinker belongs to no sect and remains outside any classification. So our second chapter will be given to these atheist philosophies and systems of thought. To their differences of style there correspond great differences in their teaching. It will be seen that the principal atheist doctrines have not arisen at random out of men's restlessness or revolt, but can be thought of as movements appealing to and rejecting one another in a story that makes sense. Hence the great question considered at the end of this second chapter: is this atheist dialectic of the mind one of expansion and fertility or one of sterile exasperation—or even of self-liquidation, if in fact atheism is unable to resolve the antinomies it develops within itself?

Contemporary atheism is not simply one philosophy among others; it is more than that. It is a culture, a way of living; it has actual existence, for Communism exerts a tyrannical authority over a whole people, their behaviour and their laws, their work and their leisure, their arts and their public life. Contemporary atheism as a mass phenomenon will be the subject of the third chapter, which will touch on the question of the meaning of contemporary history. Everything that happens has its causes stretching far into the past, and the death of God was not announced by thinkers with no roots, fallen from the *intermundia* of Epicurus. The dissolution of Christendom, the secularization and growing autonomy of science, art and politics, all tend to make a world which is *a-theist* in the literal sense of the word, that is, godless. Are not the anthropocentric humanism of the age of the middle classes, and the secularization of public life, so many forms of practical atheism? Does the present spread of a positivist and techno-logical way of thinking, inseparable from the advance of science and seeming at first sight to exclude mystery and the life within, necessarily rush mankind with the increasing momentum of a materialist and mechanistic civilization into an age without God? Is sociological atheism the truth of the modern world, the last stage of its evolution, that of its end and, perhaps, its just deserts? All these doubts can be gathered into a single fearful question: will a godless civilization irrefutably, by its experience, disprove the existence of God? Is God a political problem which history will in the end resolve?

We shall see at the end of our first three chapters that the meeting of atheism with totalitarianism in the same culture is for both the hour of testing, the hour of truth. A system of thought which proudly makes a dogma of what it calls its progressiveness can only realize itself in society in a regression towards mythology and the walled city. The movement of liberation has reawakened the ancient tyrannies. The evil being seen for what it is, it will then remain to discover how the values of the modern world and the significance of God can be reconciled within one and the same civilization. Once again, the problem is one of the philosophy of history, but it can only be truly resolved by the witness and action of

Christians and, more generally, of believers, in the actual lives of men.

A last series of questions will provide matter for our fourth chapter. Let us in the great tradition of philosophy call wisdom the regulation of man's existence in accordance with a Being or an Idea which is taken as a supreme and unsurpassable truth. It is of the essence of atheism and, if we consider it deeply, the source of its dynamic power, to call this wisdom in question. Why does atheism object to and reject God, except because God seems to it the basis of wisdom, the only wisdom, perhaps? So to end this essay we must deal with the conflict, the very revealing conflict, between atheism and wisdom.

There are different kinds of wisdom. Atheism can very usefully denounce that of an avaricious establishment, or of a God used to justify long oppression of the body and suppression of the mind. Atheist criticism can greatly help Christian thought that is too timidly self-reserved or insufficiently existential, and can make plain to such thinkers the artificiality of rationalist theodicy or the pitiable condition of man, stripped at last of his consoling mythology. But recognition that the devil occasionally helps to build has never meant that the devil was not the devil but an angel in disguise whose disciples we could cheerfully become. The valid notion of atheism as a purifying agent must itself be purged of any complacent "fellow-travelling". That Christian culture, having become such as it is, should have to pass through the fire of philosophical and political atheism to be reborn true at last after such a providential catastrophe, this is apocalyptic simple-mindedness, with more of madness in it than of reasonable thought, which we shall have good reasons for rejecting. Besides, Marxist atheism is unable to play this purifying part since, to exist in history at all, it turns back to older and retrograde ideas of wisdom, destroying, in order to build itself up, even such truth as may be found at the highest levels of atheism. To comprehend and surpass the great crisis of modern atheism, Christian wisdom does not need substantially to change its principles, or rather its spirit, untouched by time as they must be; but it must show itself more clearly to be what it already is, though sometimes only obscurely and by implication.

"... BUT ONLY TO A CERTAIN DEGREE"

On the subject of atheism Pascal said all there is to say in a famous phrase: "Atheism is an indication of spiritual vigour, but only to a certain degree."[2] We shall do justice to atheism and discover its truth if we think of it as an act of courage, or as a spiritually heroic act of will, but as cut short, as in fact retreating before the despair it causes and the contradictions it produces, until it falls back into mythology, until it destroys itself in pantheism. Untenable, intolerable unless it is that momentary nakedness of spirit familiar to the saints and mystics who know at once and together the absence and the presence of God, as the exploration of a void swept clean of all idols and pretences to plenitude, atheism can take its place within the wisdom of religion and so bear witness to a truth which makes its own reply by giving meaning, dialectically and existentially, to all man's thinking, pious or impious, and even to the dogmatics of absurdity.

We shall thus attempt to join in one exposition a fair account of atheism and a refutation of it. Neither the Catholic faith nor Christian philosophy need be afraid to relive the life and retrace the steps of atheism, for in this way the very method of Pascal is grasped and made available to our own age. It was enough for the author of *Conversations with M. de Saci* to reduce a neo-Stoic pantheism and a scepticism inclined to atheism to their essentials in terms of human personality for the problem of man to be tied up in so strict a manner that a Christian conclusion became likely, probable, even necessary—the necessity being at least practical and vital. To be inspired by a high standard which one knows one cannot reach is yet to recognize

[2] Pascal, *Pensées*, ed. Brunschvicg, III, 225; p. 431.

both one's own limitations and the exemplary value of such masters.

It is easy to distinguish a living refutation, such as that attempted here, from those systematic allegations of deception made by contemporary bigots who, using psychoanalysis as a key to unlock all doors, lay bare various sordid hidden motives and purposes when disputing ideas contrary to their own. But it is necessary to preserve the idea of refutation from the contempt in which it is held by the *misologoi*, as Plato called those who hate reason and mistrust argument; those, for example, who repeat in too facile and superficial a manner Alain's words: "In my eyes, every proof is clearly discredited." We have already, in *The God of Reason* written for this series by Régis Jolivet, a stylish and lively account of the techniques of refutation most reasonably successful against pantheism and atheism. Being convinced by it, we can agree that this refutation has the soundness of a classical system of thought. Our method seems—but properly only seems—to grant more to our opponent. It is dialectical in that it tries to use as an affirmative basis the other's negation; it is also existential, since it seeks to make out the often ambiguous meaning of historical situations and of human behaviour. But to do either is to use the idea of rational refutation, to believe in the power of the reason.

Modern atheism attains to a kind of pitch of darkness which overwhelms and destroys all religion offering intellectual or social comfort. To proclaim that God is dead is to introduce tragedy into thought as well as into existence, and the man of wisdom will only have the mastery over this tragic note in man if he sees its true value and does not deal falsely with the stark grandeur of the drama of man. God is not dead: he is the most living of all living things. But many false gods must die that the approach to the Holy of Holies be made clean.

CHAPTER I

THE TRUE SOURCE AND SOME PRETENDED ORIGINS

GOD IS NOT IMMEDIATELY EVIDENT

"There is no God above us, is the fond thought of reckless hearts" (Psalms 52. 1). This famous quotation, so often commented on by preachers and theologians, is of great importance in our context. It is there recognized that there are atheists, and therefore also that atheism is an undeniable fact of our experience. Man has the power, whether he knows what he is doing or not, to reject God and oppose wisdom. So to put forward the idea, as some apologists rashly do, that there are no atheists except in name but only "practical atheists" who through pride or idleness disregard the divine law, would be, at least at the beginning of the argument, a rhetorical convenience or an emotional prejudice evading the real question. Even if atheism is forced by its own logic to imply the suicide of the spirit, the self-destruction of man, nevertheless it certainly exists, psychologically, historically and culturally. It may be a scandal, often concealed and suppressed by social pressures, but it has become increasingly explicit and aggressive in our own times. This scandal is a fact which needs to be explained by its own causes, to be understood for what it is. Hence there arises a first question, though one by no means now arising for the first time: how can a man be an atheist? Or, more philosophically, how is atheism possible?

It is always easy to answer by appealing in an uninspired fashion to the thousand and one forms of human wickedness and stupidity. Yet the permanent, proximate and always effective cause of atheism is simply the fact that God is not immediately evident, either to the senses or to the intellect. No one can see God except by dying, either with the eyes of the body or by the vision of the soul. The condition of the flesh and the spatio-temporal law which are the determinate features of his destiny forbid man's meeting God face to face, forbid the direct perception of the Infinite and Eternal, the intuition of the Absolute.

Not that in relation to the problem of God the human reason is senseless, paralysed, incapable of reaching a positive conclusion. On the contrary, it is just the absence of direct intuition which sets the powers of the mind to work, and that not without hope of arriving at a certain truth about which the only sure thing is that it cannot be intuitive. To reach by the reason the conclusion that God exists is to know rather than to see. Every "way" towards God, to use St Thomas Aquinas' term, has some obliqueness and indirectness. Catholic tradition, made quite clear in the declaration of the Vatican Council, holds that the existence of God is demonstrable, but demonstrable by a proof that is metaphysical, that is, neither of mathematics nor of physics, one which uses all the resources of man, the spiritual aiding the intellectual, all the resources of the whole man facing the whole human situation. We should be careful not to add to these classic ideas the false corollary that atheism is impossible, or that it can be reduced at once to an absurdity.

On the contrary, the purpose of that proof, which is a kind of interior discourse in the mind, the purpose of that way, as Aquinas said, using a word so well fitted to man's itinerant state, to *homo viator*, is to fill the gap left by an intuition which is lacking or impossible. The difficult road which leads to God opens out before every man capable of reasoning for himself and of reflecting on the affirmation of existence natural to all thought; but the whole length of the journey is not imposed as an absolutely compelling necessity on each and every man. For every path that reaches its goal, how many fruitless blind alleys there are, how many lose their way! And, most important, the possibility of sudden enlightenment is necessarily excluded by the inevitable need to rely on reasoned demonstration.

Nor must the faith of the believer, which infinitely surpasses the level of human reasoning, be confused with the untroubled and transparent clarity of visible proof, even when it is made alive by a sense of God's presence. The witness of the saints and the most certain pronouncements of mystical theology prohibit the confusion of the soul's experience of God made possible by grace with the vision of the divine essence. God is there, it is true, "nearer to me than my own body", as Leibniz said; but he is there as it were as a fearful yet sweet presence on the other side of a wall, a wall with neither door nor window, which cannot be pierced or passed except through the ultimate suffering of death. Even the brightness of mystical vision and union cannot destroy the nature of faith, which even on these heights keeps something of its night, that "dark night of the soul" which the saints have likened to the crucifixion.

If God is immediately evident neither to reason rightly directed nor to faith, be it the wisest and saintliest, we can more easily understand how atheism is a permanent possibility for man, a possibility bound up with the passivity and finitude of our nature. If the "reckless hearts" of the Psalmist, who go so far as absolutely to deny the Absolute, are able to find followers in every age, it is because true wisdom lacks clear and obvious evidence and because its power over the human heart is not invincible. Atheism thus produces and supports more atheism; it becomes a reason for doubting and denying; it uses in its support the apparent evidence against God that he himself seems to have built into the working of the world. In short, God is for the human mind not an evident truth but a terrible problem which needs patient and hard work to be solved.

St Thomas takes care to show that the idea that God is

immediately evident is false right at the beginning of his *Summa Theologica*,[1] which is an indication of his rigorous and honest accuracy. Like St Anselm, he quotes the text which stands at the head of this chapter. But for him, the most scientific of theologians, the simple fact of atheism is itself sufficient to establish an important preliminary conclusion: God is not immediately knowable in and for himself, for if God were immediately evident there would be no atheists. A stricter philosophical argument confirms this commonsense inference. If the mind could ascertain the reality of God simply by perceiving it, for example by seeing clearly in the idea of perfection the necessity of his existence, then the contrary of the proposition, "God exists", could not even be formulated; it would collapse under the very weight of its own enunciation. But experience denies the truth of this conclusion: however superable the atheist's denial may be, it formulates an idea which is not immediately self-contradictory and is conceivable by men. God is only immediately evident in and for himself as pure Spirit, but not for us, spirits benighted by the flesh.

So the atheist according to St Thomas is not the reckless heart who would fondly deny the daylight in the blaze of the noonday sun, whom the apologist could push in front of him like a cheerful, drunken helot. *Utrum Deus sit* is a problem which is stark and real, and to ask the question is by no means simply a trick for teaching purposes, except in so far as teaching methods may correspond to the natural movement of the mind. Does God exist? The question is itself shrouded in mystery, for if it is seriously asked it puts the "yes" and "no" into the balance. So to discuss the existence of God is reasonable,

[1] *Summa Theologica, Pars prima*, qu. II, art. 1: St Thomas, in asking whether God is knowable in himself, *per se notum*, sets out to refute the argument of St Anselm, later to be famous as the "ontological argument". And in fact, if this argument contains a concealed appeal to intuition and is bound up with an "ontologism" or illuminationism, Christian philosophy must judge it difficult to accept. But there are other interpretations of the ontological argument which are compatible with the notion that God is not immediately evident, and the discussion is still open on this most important point.

and the possibility of atheism is thus established by the analysis of the problem itself. Battle can then be joined and objections found to objections in order to deny the atheist's denial. But the hope that atheism be presumed susceptible to refutation implies that the enemy does exist and is not without intelligence. A rational argument cannot refute what is a denial of reason, but only another rational argument, and it is as a rational system of thought that atheism will be refutable. The *Summa* has sized up the enemy exactly.

THE TWO SOURCES OF ATHEISM

So atheism has its rational basis and can be organized, if not into a system, at least as a coherent doctrine. When St Thomas considers the question, *utrum Deus sit*,[2] he does not try to avoid the necessity to state the case for the opposition. Now this case is twofold, so that St Thomas distinguishes two sources of atheism, one in reflection on our knowing, the other in meditation on existence; both arise from the fundamental lack of immediate evidence of God.

The human mind, says St Thomas, is capable of objective knowledge, properly scientific knowledge, which advances in its proper field and attains to truth without meeting God at the beginning, in its progress or at the end. Natural phenomena have their own laws which are sufficient to them and sufficient to the mind. The conduct, or if one prefer it, the behaviour of man, a rational animal, is explicable in terms of ends, of principles, or again laws, which need not be referred to a beyond, but which are immanent in the nature of man. Only nature and man, intelligible in themselves and capable of being endlessly explored, can speak for nature and man. The "other", the transcendent, this is a problem which does not arise for science as such. The scientist tempted by atheism, because in his investigation and interpretation of the world he "has no need of that hypothesis", God, is not only inevitably

2 *Summa Theologica, Pars prima*, qu. II, art. 3.

typical of our times, but is to be found and is faced by St Thomas in the opening pages of the *Summa*.

On the other hand,[3] if science does not produce "any necessity for positing God's existence",[4] the fact of evil visible in the world is a good reason compelling us to deny the existence of an invisible God. To raise this objection to the level of the intellect it is best to pass beyond the sickness and dullness of mind produced by unhappiness, wickedness and death, the ever-renewed forms of evil in the world; for nothing more than evil induces a man to think wrongly and fall into revolt and denial. So St Thomas grants to his opponent the advantage of an argumentation the more difficult to refute because metaphysically strict. If God is the Good, infinite and unlimited, does not evil seem to be, to use the language of Plato's *Theaetetus*, the opposite of God? But if there is an opposite of God, does not this limited and opposed God immediately and thereby cease to be God? How can this Being who, in a world for which he accepts the whole responsibility, supports the presence and action of his own antithesis, his very opposite, how can he still be called God, when his essence is contradicted and his power checked? Either God is not God, or evil, which runs so free a course through the world, to use again the words of the *Theaetetus*, is not evil. To hold at the same time that God exists and that evil is real seems at first sight an impossibility for our reason. A syllogism formulated by St Thomas sets forth this most stubborn objection, which from age to age has taken such different shapes, learned or popular: if God existed, evil would not be found

[3] For the convenience of my own exposition I have reversed St Thomas' order; he puts the objection raised by the fact of evil first and then considers secondly, in his *videtur quod*, that raised by the metaphysical and religious neutrality of man's science, proceeding from the more to the less important of the atheist's arguments. But I have followed the letter and the spirit of the text, though modernizing the form of expression here and there.

[4] *Nulla igitur necessitas est ponere Deum esse* (*Summa Theologica, Pars prima*, qu. II, art. 3, *videtur quod*).

anywhere; but evil is found in the world; therefore God does not exist.[5]

The old, medieval texts we have just recalled have an astonishingly contemporary air. The claim of science to complete independence and autonomy, and the distress caused by evil, which becomes first criticism, then denial: these are the two sources of atheism. They are not passing phases but permanent features. Nor were they discovered by our own irreligious times, for the intellectual honesty of a great thirteenth-century theologian set them out with as much vigour as clarity. Already in the *Summa Theologica* we find a lot of the fundamental ideas and justificatory arguments which were to be used by the most famous modern atheists to convince themselves that God is dead. St Thomas used the phraseology and imagery of an age and a culture different from our own to give his account of atheism and its refutation, but the strictness of his argumentation is not thereby weakened: its lines can be clearly seen beneath the period costume it happens to wear. This is because atheism does not belong to any particular period of history. This must be stressed right at the beginning of a study of contemporary atheism: the motives and movements which give rise to and encourage atheism exist less in this or that kind of culture than in the nature and condition of man, man confronted at once by the success of his scientific inquiry into nature and the failure of his reflection on what exists, from which evil cannot be excluded. Science, the only mistress of his rational processes, accounts for more and more of the universe, fact after fact, phenomenon after phenomenon: so God is unnecessary. Evil is *a-theist*, godless or even exclusive of God, since by the very fact that it *is*, it forbids us to postulate

---

[5] *Si ergo Deus esset, nullum malum inveniretur. Invenitur autem malum in mundo. Ergo Deus non est (Summa Theologica, Pars prima,* qu. II, art. 3, *videtur quod).* The reader is referred to the refutations proposed by St Thomas of an atheism the nature of which he has so admirably set forth: refutations at once Aristotelian and Augustinian which, considered as to their matter, belong more to their own times than the account of atheism that goes before them.

an absolute Good: so God is impossible. These are the twin attacks made by atheists today.

The originality of contemporary atheism can therefore properly be denied. For modern atheism can justly be summed up in the phrase: God is scientifically unnecessary and ethically impossible. Science knows nothing of God, and so denies his existence; so runs the argument of that atheism called scientific, which makes a metaphysics of physics. Since there is evil in the world, no recourse to an absolute or perfect being can justify existence; so says that other atheism we call existentialist, according to which an existence, apprehended in and apart from ourselves as absurd, proves that the order of the universe is not the moral order it ought to be if God existed. The best "phenomenology" of contemporary atheism is thus summed up in a few lines of the *Summa Theologica*.

That God is scientifically unnecessary is an idea common to Auguste Comte and to Karl Marx. For the founder of positivism, law, the necessary relation between facts, contains the only truth about the world. The gods, and God—for he is only a metaphysical abstraction from the gods—represent a kind of explanation which, necessary at first, was surpassed directly the mind, awakened and informed by science, entered step by step, slowly but irrevocably, the age of positivism. Sociology, the highest of the sciences, the accomplishment of the positivist age, explains by its laws, and first by the famous law of the three stages of civilization, the process of the history of human society, at last understood and properly ordered. Progress is only the development of an order entirely implicit in human nature, and only in human nature, which is realized throughout history. Whoever persists in introducing into the interplay of natural conditions and social purposes a transcendent Author or an almighty Actor, destroys all scientific thought and shows himself a reactionary enemy of that modern knowledge and wisdom which Comte called sociology, which is in fact a political philosophy of history. Between the horizontal chain of phenomenal causes and the vertical chain of divine causality the opposition is absolute and irreconcilable. What is relative is absolutely incompatible with what is absolute. Law does away with God. Once human history is made scientific by the power of sociology, positivism has no more to do than sign the death certificate of God.

For the inventor of dialectical materialism atheism is the condition of the possibility of science and, more especially, of scientific history, as it was for Auguste Comte. The assertion of materialism means, in Marxist terms, that matter—which broadly and without analysing it means nature, the world, reality—contains in itself the laws of its own development, laws this time called dialectical, because new syntheses are supposed to arise from the creative conflicts and contradictions of thesis and antithesis. All natural things including men contain intrinsic principles and causes of their movements and growth, of the progress of the whole. "Autodynamism" is the word used by Communist textbooks and catechisms; for the understanding of Marxism it is a key word, which means that nature and history, sufficient in themselves and self-explanatory, destroy with one blow the illusions of the supernatural and the transhistoric. For example, the class war, scientifically determinable itself, is the moving force in history, and it leads to the promised land—the rationally promised land—of a classless society, a humanity which is, thanks to the death of God, itself its own providence.

So, whether positivist or materialist, modern atheism speaks precisely the same language: make God the master of the natural world, and there is no natural world; make God the prime mover in history and there is no history. These two ideas, which have so much influence on contemporary thought, are at bottom really only one. Their origin, their seminal reason, can be expressed as a principle of immanence, that principle St Thomas sets out when he is considering the foundations of atheism: the phenomena of nature are reducible to a causality which is natural; the phenomena of human behaviour are reducible to a causality which is human, man's reason and will.[6] Nature immanent in nature, man immanent in man, these are claims made by a knowledge which is only really to be called scientific once science has won its independence. The development of the sciences since St Thomas has produced many examples of this idea, which is in itself neither ancient nor modern but in a way classical: the reclamation for scientific knowledge of the immanence of nature. God is not a fact in nature along with and like other facts; God is not a character in history fitting into the story, into the interplay of human and material causes. From the fact that God is fundamentally unnecessary to science, atheism draws the conclusion that it is experimentally and rationally proved that God does not exist. This is bad logic, and we shall see that it is confusing and mystifying. In the *videtur quod* of St Thomas, as in positivism and Marxism, atheism reveals the identity and the persistence of one of its fundamental principles.

God is, then, scientifically unnecessary; he is also ethically impossible. This is the characteristic note of contemporary existentialism. Today, a number of provocative and startling ideas are expressed in the forms where philosophy and literature meet, in essays, in plays, in metaphysical treatises. In them is broadcast an atheism which has a modern air about it: being which has no purpose, which is superfluous in eternity; art as the only permanent currency of a mythical absolute; mind which invents gratuitous values in an infinite, valueless universe. This kind of atheism borrows the most varied notions, speaking of anxiety, of dread, of the senselessness of the world, or rather of man in the world, and never stops probing, harassing, ravaging the conscience of our time. Malraux,

---

6 I have almost literally translated St Thomas' text: *ea quae sunt naturalia reducuntur in principium quod est natura; ea vero quae sunt a proposito reducuntur in principium quod est ratio humana vel voluntas. (Summa Theologica, Pars prima,* qu. ii, art. 3, *videtur quod.)* A modern atheist might reply that in St Thomas the principle of immanence is more metaphysical than positivist; but St Thomas may well have brought out in this text the metaphysics inherent in all positivism.

Sartre, Camus, each has his own problems, his own style, but all are sliding down the same slope: between the world, brute and meaningless fact as it is, and the human mind, alive, weightless, instinct with the demands of reason and of justice, the gap is inevitable, the breach irreparable. That is the axiom, the fundamental postulate of this school of thought. Recourse to a God as principle of all things and creator of the natural world and of man would introduce into the world an imaginary and consoling harmony which the simple apprehension of the senselessness of the whole is sufficient to prove false. In other words, the break between man and the world is such that there could not be any unity between them other than poetic, but when poetry is taken for truth, how can it be called anything other than magic or superstition? So for Paul Valéry, the father—undeniably the father, though seldom recognized as such—of many of the most important existentialist ideas, religion only humanizes a world which is infra- or even anti-human, by basely giving in to the idolatries of the heart. So man can only maintain his honour—and this is the core of existentialist ethics—by rejecting the mythologies which reconcile man and the world, and by resigning himself to the discomfort of permanently being in protest, in denying the world which denies him, in replying to a blind negation with a negation which is conscious and ever renewed, and which presents itself in the philosophy of some modern writers as the essential act of a free being.

To state it still more briefly, existentialist man cannot morally give his assent to the world as it is. It is thus easy to see that the substance of this position is the same as the ancient objection on the grounds that evil exists, but it has become more keenly passionate, more eloquent and lyrical, and is rooted more deeply in experience. But at bottom it is still and always the same.

Why indeed is it laid down that the unity of the world cannot be discovered, except because it is different, very different, from a spiritual and moral harmony? We are faced by a universe which goes its way according to laws blind and indifferent to our purposes, even the most unselfish; a world which, for example, gives existence to man and then takes it back again with no regard to the good which the mind can irrefutably claim. Over and over again it is said, in a thousand ways, not all of them in tune with the others, that man cannot, simply by virtue of his dignity as a thinking being, assent to the condition he finds himself in. The reason, the quite obvious reason, is that he carries in himself an imperative moral need which is not only frustrated but contradicted by things as they are, and which he cannot finally satisfy except by an act of heroism, in a way that is precarious, contingent and as it were symbolic. The consciousness we may briefly and conveniently call existentialist is thus a moral consciousness which is stirred up, aware by an interior conviction of absolute good. Since there is in the world the very opposite of that good, ineradicable evil, the absolute good is condemned, as long as there is a living consciousness, to remain an unfulfilled need that never has existence. For if this absolute good were real, it would at once make the world and man an ethical whole. So we come back to the *videtur quod* of St Thomas and the second perennial source of atheism. A truly existing God, as Alain said—the other unacknowledged but recognizable master of atheist existentialism—would by his existence assume the responsibility for and the justification of evil: so there is no absolute Good, there is no God. A world in which there is evil is, precisely, God-less.

So we can draw a preliminary conclusion: there is nothing radically original about contemporary atheism. It is not as if mankind, or some pioneers of man's advance, thanks to a deepening of his scientific knowledge or some decisive progress in his ethical thinking, had discovered that God was merely a myth created by a mind dormant and unenlightened; or as if modern man at last possessed definitive and irrefutable proof that God does not exist, before which the old theologies and traditional apologetics find themselves defenceless. This is a misconception we have now got rid of. Even if they are not completely rational, the reasons that justify the atheist are potentially there in the mind of man, when he is brought up against his own capacity to know and to act. Since my science, as science, can never enable me to find him, and arrives at true conclusions without introducing him into the argument, is not God unnecessary? Since the world and my experience of it irrefutably convince me of the existence of evil, is not God ethically, and therefore metaphysically, impossible? All atheism, ancient or modern, must arise from one or other of these two questions, and St Thomas' *videtur quod* is surely confirmed in a remarkable way by the two faces, the one positivist, the other existentialist, of contemporary atheism.

CONTEMPORARY ATHEISM IS A KIND OF HUMANISM

So in all forms of atheism we find the same lines of argument, the same fundamental structure. Yet it is true that all contemporary atheists have their own proper and immediately recognizable character, whatever the differences of content in their teachings or of style in their attitudes. Whether they are triumphant or despairing, they seek in the denial of God the total affirmation of man. Atheism marks itself out as a form of humanism, and claims to have itself brought man to the limit of his powers and capabilities. Hence the presupposition that belief in God is, inversely, a sort of dehumanizing of man. This is the common ground, in all senses of the word, of contemporary atheists. This humanist note, in which lies the real originality of modern atheism, cannot be derived from or explained by the preceding account and analysis. We must therefore try to describe this humanism before we look for its source.

First, it is easy to gather together a few quotations which clearly illustrate this aspect of atheism. Marx's essay "On

German Ideology" played a determining, and even an origi-
nating, part in the growth of Marxism. In that work the problem
of God is reduced to a human problem. The only meaning
there is in the adventure of man lies in his achievement of
complete independence. But man, according to Marx, "can
only be his own master when he owes his existence to no one
but himself".[7] God the Creator would thus destroy this
complete self-mastery man aspires to. To owe one's livelihood
to someone else is already to be unbearably dependent;
but that the very source of life itself should be someone else,
that the reason for my existence should be beyond and above
me, means that I do not exist of myself but am condemned to
eternal servitude, in this world and the next. So the salvation of
man itself demands, as it were *a priori*, the death of God.
According to Marx, as soon as I ask myself about God, as
soon as I seek an external, different principle of my own
existence, then I begin to dehumanize myself, to consent to
my own estrangement or alienation, to use an idea fundamental
to Marxism which is most significantly introduced in this essay.
For then, since I was made from what was not, I suppose
myself originally not existing, "I abstract from my humanity",[8]
which is clearly to offend against humanism, to destroy myself
on the ideal level before enslaving myself to an idol. Humanity
will only be free when men are convinced that they owe their
existence to no one beyond mankind. Now "for socialist man,
all the so-called history of the world is only the production of
man by men's labour".[9] That labour, by which man constructs
himself as man, is thus the irrefutable proof that man is his
own originator. We shall meet this idea again, this antithesis
between creation, with its mystery, and labour, which sets men
free. It is perhaps the germ of the whole of Marxism. Each of
these, creation and labour, is the inverse of the other in human

[7] Karl Marx. *Economie politique et philosophie. Idéologie allemande* (Ire
partie); written in 1845; Molitor trans., p. 38.
[8] *Op. cit.*, p. 39.
[9] *Op. cit.*, p. 40.

consciousness, the first decreasing in proportion as the second grows, until one day labour will be all and creation nothing. In the same essay, thanks to the light that comes from labour, Marx gives us the perfect, simple epitome of atheist humanism: "Atheism is a denial of God, and by this denial man's existence is asserted."[10]

In very much the same language and at about the same time, Auguste Comte said much the same thing. Understanding by religion an achievement of man's own which released and satisfied both the powers of his mind and those of his heart, and wanting to reconcile once for all religion and positivism, Comte resolved to get rid of God altogether as irreligious. The "slave of God" of the theological ages was a man stunted and diminished, a still uncertain seed of the men to come. The "servant of humanity" of the age of positivism was to come into full possession of the nature of man. As opposed to Marx, Comte allowed that God, or rather the idea of God in the mind of man, had a certain usefulness, as it were for instruction and formation during the childhood and slow maturing of our species. But now, God could be no more than an obstacle on the path of progress. His "regency" ended when the kingdom of man began.

Nietzsche was not looking for the fulfilment of man through the death of God, since for Zarathustra man himself was to be surpassed. But for him, as for Comte, it was God who prevented the superman growing in man, who condemned man to remain indefinitely as he was. If God exists, then whatever the inequalities of appearance, of status, of circumstances, all men are equal before him, all are equally dependent. Only when the false sun of God is set below the horizon can the star of the superman rise. So Zarathustra: "Ye higher men, this God was your greatest danger. Only since he lay in the grave have ye again arisen. Now only cometh the great noontide, now only doth the higher man become—master! . . . Now only

10 Karl Marx, *Economie politique et philosophie. Idéologie allemande* (Ire partie); written in 1845; Molitor trans., p. 40.

travaileth the mountain of the human future. God hath died: now do *we* desire—the Superman to live."[11] But even if the word "humanist" can hardly be applied to Nietzsche (we ought perhaps rather to speak of a kind of blazing forth of man towards the superman), yet the most startling prophet of atheism who has appeared in the history of thought saw in the death of God the necessary if not sufficient condition for humanity, in a few privileged individuals, to be marvellously ennobled, so that man should be borne beyond himself towards a remote, unheard-of possibility that Nietzsche spoke of only in symbols, in images, in parables—in a word, prophetically.

This same idea, of the deliverance or advancement of man made possible by the death or the forgetting of God, is there also in more modern writers. There is in Freudian psychology a kind of debased and murky shadow of Nietzsche's ideas. Man, who committed in the mythical but ever-present and pressing past that mysterious crime Freud calls "the murder of the Father", cannot overcome his own remorse, cannot return to the time before this original sin, because the Father is truly dead; but man is also incapable of commending himself for abolishing for ever the Father's kingdom. So all human psychology is based on a fundamental neurosis, and is thus unstable and contradictory. Clearly, man as Freud describes him is an irrevocably aborted Nietzschean superman! According to Freud, the death of God is meaningless except as a promise of a complete humanism, which is itself ultimately impossible and bound to be frustrated. So Freud is another good example of the dialectics of modern atheism; they are to be found also in the works of Malraux and Sartre.

Putting these two names together might perhaps offend the author of *The Metamorphosis of the Gods*, and it is true that Malraux has never called himself an atheist in the frankly ostentatious manner that is Sartre's own. But fundamentally,

---

[11] *Thus Spake Zarathustra;* trans. T. Common, vol. 11 of complete works, ed. O. Levy; London, George Allen & Unwin, and New York, Macmillan; 5th edn, 1923, p. 351.

in the last analysis, for the one as for the other, man only becomes man by freeing himself from the Absolute. The distinction, which is not that of common usage, which Malraux draws between the sacred or holy and the divine, has just this implication. When he passionately inquires into great and universal works of art it is to find there at times a religion of the Absolute, one which turns all to stone and fixes it immovably, making of man a mummy tightly wrapped in the bands of holiness, and at times a clear, brisk humanism, which leaps in triumph and in its freedom of movement makes godlike the forms, figures and actions of men. Hindu temples, Byzantine basilicas, Romanesque churches, these come into the category of the holy: Greek temples, Gothic art, sculpture and architecture, these reveal the divine. Man only discovers himself in triumphing over this obsession with the eternal, in rejecting the holy and reacting towards the divine: to a divine which means that God is dead.

To end this brief but none the less useful list, Sartre hardly believes in a glorious kingdom of man on earth: he is nearer Nietzsche than Marx, and nearer Freud than Nietzsche, for Sartre's man has killed God precisely for nothing—or rather for nothingness, for he then lives in absolute freedom, the empty vanity of nothingness. But right from the beginning of Sartre's thought these two complementary ideas are there, the denial of God and the birth of man, with a brute strength and firmness which brushes aside tact and caution. As soon as man discovers in his despair that his freedom belongs only to itself, and that it discovers and maintains only those values which give a precarious meaning to life, he knows that God does not exist; for if God existed he would, like Malraux's holiness, immobilize, paralyse, petrify freedom, which should be lively and active.

So man only seeks and finds God from cowardice, in order to escape his responsibility, which he knows to be total but does not want to recognize, or in order to absorb his independence in a dependence which enables him to escape from himself.

Let a man realize that he is condemned to be a man, that there is no prayer, no worship, no devotion which can release him from being painfully and absolutely free, and God will no longer exist, he will be killed by the awakened consciousness of man.

In every case, then, abortive or successful, triumphant or despairing, contemporary atheism is a kind of humanism. It is seen to be less a conclusion that sums up an exhaustive inquiry in a negation, than an initial decision. In the end it all comes to a sort of *cogito*, a sort of first principle that completely excludes God. If I think as a free man, I am the only source, and in a single act of intuition I see that God is useless and impossible: I am, therefore there is no God. That is the logical order of proof. There is no God, therefore I am, is the phenomenological order of discovery. These are propositions valid for the kinds of nineteenth- and twentieth-century atheism we have just described. We now have to inquire whether this atheist humanism is original, and what was its origin.

IN THE BEGINNING WAS HEGEL

Before Sartre, Nietzsche or Marx, a writer of mediocre genius but enormous influence, Feuerbach, seems to have been the first to set the tone of more than a century of atheist philosophy by making God the myth that destroys man's own efforts, against which man must fight to reconquer his proper nature, from which he has been alienated. God is for Feuerbach "merely the projected essence of Man", and "in proportion as God becomes more ideally human, the greater becomes the apparent difference between God and Man. To enrich God, man must become poor; that God may be all, man must become nothing".[12]

So man can only grow and enrich himself by taking back

[12] L. Feuerbach, *The Essence of Christianity* (trans. George Eliot), ed. and abridged by E. Graham Waring and F. W. Strothmann, New York, Harper, 1957; pp. 65, 16.

what he has given to God; the dawn of man supposes the twilight of God. Now Feuerbach was one of the "left-wing Hegelians", and we may doubt whether without Hegel the author of *The Essence of Christianity* would have so precisely formulated modern atheism.

Hegel stands in fact on the threshold of our own age like a mountain—like Nietzsche's "mountain of the human future", which travailed to bring forth a whole future for man, philosophical and cultural, intellectual and political. Marxism grew out of Hegelianism, for Marx reasoned only according to a dialectic that came to him from Hegel. All his vision of the past of man and of the movement of history was derived from that great inventor Hegel, so well able to comprehend the course of history in one simple and sweeping glance. If some of the founders of Communism have sometimes violently attacked Hegelian philosophy, their hostility is that of healthy and well-fed infants who hit out at their nurse, of ex-pupils so closely attached to and possessed by the thought of their master that they have a vague grudge against him because of their dependence on him, and can therefore only express their own personalities by taking arms against him who formed them. Yet despite this reversal of meaning, it remains the same thought, developed, applied, and perhaps even realized.

The way things begin always determines the way they develop, and the Hegelian beginnings of Marxism determined its course not only as a philosophy but also as a code for man's dealings with his fellows, and as the motivating principle of a culture that is more totalitarian even than materialist, in the ordinary sense of the word. But Hegelianism was not wholly absorbed into Marxism, which is at once the same thing and its antithesis, to use, as is here especially fitting, the terms of the Hegelian dialectic. Both by its direct and its indirect influence, by the lively reaction it produced—first and foremost in Kierkegaard— Hegelianism determined the course of a century and a half of Western philosophy, driving it to both extremes, of rationalism and irrationalism. No other thinker, not even Aristotle, who is comparable in stature, in his encyclopedic scope, and in his influence far beyond his own circle and time, no one has had such power, such tyrannical power, over the thought of others as Hegel. Today, in this *diaspora* of philosophies each of which rejects or even completely ignores all the others, none of them can escape its Hegelian heritage, just as modern nations that have only recently come somewhat unsteadily into separate existence must wittingly or unwittingly, nostalgically or resentfully, acknowledge their debt to the Empire that in its own fall gave them birth. Lastly, and most important, Hegel sowed at the beginning of our own age the seed, the terrible seed, of totalitarianism, dressed in the trappings of high philosophy, and so profoundly influenced the development of our times, so much so that the twentieth century is in many ways a Hegelian century. By a paradox which is good evidence for the primacy of the mind, although Hegel's ideas were protected from the practical curiosity of the layman by the severe technicality and subtle art of the most difficult of the philosophers, nevertheless they have had a great and determining influence on the actual course of history, on the fate of actual men and women.

Yet this same Hegel whom we can expect to find at the heart of all forms of modern atheism is the very opposite of an atheist. Few philosophers have made more of God, even to the point of systematically taking the side of the infinite and absolute against the littleness of individual men. But Hegel, and this is surely the basis of his teaching, judged that the story of man, in which he thought that Christianity had its proper and necessary place, could not be rationally completed except by passing beyond Christianity. He also called in question the God of Christian experience, who becomes in his philosophy an inadequate and mutilated image, premature and overhastily formed, of the only true God, who gradually and completely reveals himself in conceptual clarity through the whole course of history. To rescue religious belief from the vague twilight of imagery and from riddling symbolism, and to transform it, having ended for ever the age of parables, into rational

knowledge about men and the world, this was the revolution of
which Hegel intended so resolutely to make himself the prophet,
this is what makes Hegelianism, the philosophy of that revolution, a unique example of autocratic philosophy, of intellectual
despotism, of a tyrannical system. To put the matter briefly,
Hegel undertook to reform the God of Christian experience,
so that history could attain to its rational completion. From
this reformation other consequences follow, which are the
principal forms taken by atheism today.

A God who can only be experienced or thought of when the
conscience is sick: this, says Hegel, is the actual God of Christians as he is found in history, the opponent of the light of
reason. He is first the God of the Jews, infinitely above all
nature and all human society, self-sufficient and absolute,
willing the existence of the world and of man only by an act of
will entirely free and contingent; a first principle so perfectly
existing that his creation adds absolutely nothing to his being;
the God, that is, of unapproachable transcendence, but also
the God of inscrutable mystery, impossible to represent in the
imagination or comprehend in the intellect; a God before
whom the problem of man can only be expressed in terms of the
alternative, so obnoxious to true freedom, between obedience
and revolt. Now transcendence and mystery arouse in the heart
of man an aspiration that cannot be fulfilled, but is for ever
humbled in its powerlessness. It follows that the fullness of
God can only be glorified by the emptying out of man, by
man's consciousness of his own wretched nothingness. So
religion is a sad attempt to be as little as possible and to depend
as much as possible. A transcendent God of mystery reduces
man to a condition of servitude and alienation, since what
matters most, what possesses all being and all value, is absolutely beyond his grasp. Transcendence and mystery make God a
tyrant over man, and so there must be established between
God and man, grim and inevitable as fate, the famous dialectic
of master and slave.

At first the New Testament seems to be the Good News that

sets man free, victorious over fate, which will purify the religious concepts now released from the master-slave dialectic.
Should not transcendence be done away with, now that the
absolute has become man, and appeared as one of us, now that
the unapproachable is known as our nearest neighbour is
known? Once the mystery of God is revealed in Christ does
it not cease to be a mystery, since it has become a word of
truth the mind can understand, a teaching of love the heart can
feel? And now that the old night of transcendence and mystery
has given place to a new dawn, has not the time come—as the
young Hegel believed for a brief space—for a reconciliation of
man and God which should signify the end of the unhappy
conscience?

A vain hope, a Hegel more like himself was to say later. A
God bound up in a precarious and fleeting sensible existence,
disappearing as soon as he appears, he also dooms to unhappiness the heart enchanted by him. The most precious, the most
divine and perfect, existed in a particular and privileged here
and now: thenceforth there is no here and now that does not
find them missing, the most precious, the most perfect, the
divine. Only traces are left of the passage of the Lord, ambiguous
traces, effaceable and effaced; the memory of his disciples,
parables difficult to interpret, an empty tomb. The believer
will wear himself out in vain trying to bring back to life the
presence screened and hidden by the false memorial of ceremony, the ineffectual symbolism of ritual. So the incarnation
of God only founds a backward-looking religion, a religion of
waiting without end. The heart and mind faithful to Christ are
only mournful and sickly versions of the heart and mind in
submission to the God of Israel: they are devoted to their tears
and their incurable grief. The stark transcendence of the Jews
is not suppressed, it only becomes distant, undefined and vague;
the divine mystery is not penetrated, but seeming to reveal
itself fleetingly and enigmatically it really takes the wavering
form of an elusive ambiguity. The Christian conscience
is only that of the Jew, such that a doleful poetry cannot

change it essentially. The "unhappy conscience" tends to become the "beautiful soul", endowed with a romantic religiosity, eternally betrothed to the unreal and the impossible, always aspiring further, elsewhere. In vain is the unhappiness reduced and refined: it is neither dissolved away nor surpassed.

The liberation of man is the greater failure since Christianity, refusing to break away from the legacy of Israel, preserved alongside of one another reverence for the God of the old Law and devotion to the God of the New Testament. Hence the Judaeo-Christian heart must live in separation from God: this is the cross it must carry. The Christian must say again and again, to increase his unhappiness, that the world is apart from God and that God is beyond the world; that Christ came into the world, but his own neither knew nor received him. The Christian must live in this vale of tears like an exile, suffering the torture of the saints. According to Hegel, the poet's phrase, "we are not in the world", perfectly expresses the condition brought upon man by a God only partially revealed, a God stubbornly transcendent and mysterious. So we can see the fundamental opposition between Hegel and anyone in the Judaeo-Christian tradition: be his name Isaias or Kant, he cannot really act and live as a true son or king of the earth, for he never ceases to condemn the ways of the world, he is ever aflame with the hope for something else, rejecting what he can know and hold and be grateful for. For him the stream of history is like the waters of Babylon, beside which, like the exiled Jews, he dreams constantly of the unattainable Jerusalem. To use the words of Hegel himself, the Christian can be a witness, a martyr, but he can never be a "hero of action"; the glory of Prometheus or Faust is forbidden to him. So Hegel inferred the social and historical end to Christianity: even if it changed some individual men's lives, by teaching them asceticism or the inner life of the spirit, yet it could never build such a great cooperative work as a society, a civilization. To produce in any age souls firmly withdrawn from their age is not to give a spirit to an age. The desert which endlessly surrounds the chosen, the elect, between Egypt and the Promised Land; the temple on Mount Sion destroyed by the people of the flesh; the cross whereon the just One died, unknown, misunderstood; the empty tomb of crusade and pilgrimage and heartsickness; these are the symbols in which the Judaeo-Christian heart seeks a nourishment all too spiritual, confesses its soul, and tries in the dim light of faith to see God's presence in the emptiness of its withdrawal from the world.

Judaeo-Christianity lacks, if one may believe Hegel, what formed the light and power of Hellenism: that sense of the permeation of the world by divinity which prevented any opposition between nature and God, and that total commitment to the city-state which made the real, the true man the citizen. Judaeo-Christianity is in Hegel's dialectic the antithesis of that earlier thesis, and to discover the absoluteness and the holiness of the soul is to call in question nature and the city-state. Though such a testing experience was necessary, it could not produce harmony and stability. Man's future, now informed by a profoundly disturbing movement to pass beyond its present state, cannot rest in Judaeo-Christianity, but tends inevitably towards a third stage, to use Comte's terminology, a stage heralded and ushered in by that synthesis of Hellenism and Christianity, united with such power in him, ultra-pagan as he was and ultra-Christian, which constitutes the whole basis of Hegel's philosophy.

This philosophy finally puts an end to the time of enigma and parable, of image and symbol. In the last analysis, Hegelianism is nothing other than a completely rational interpretation of the Christian Scriptures. At the very centre is the death of God, the tragedy of Good Friday, which cast down the Christian heart into everlasting agony. It is true, it is indeed rationally certain, that God is dead. But this hard saying must be understood and changed into something beyond Christianity for the soul to have joy of it. God is dead the moment the world and human history exist; for, passing into its opposite, the absolute becomes relative, the infinite becomes finite, the eternal, temporal. Conceived on their own, creation and incarnation are obscure dogmas that torture the spirit with agonizing mystery; conceived together, they reveal to the spirit set free the contradiction that is the secret of God. The day of the creation and the day of the death of God are one and the same day. God loses himself in the world and in history, dies to himself in order to find himself alive again in drawing together the world and history into one whole. So that by working in the world and acting in history we are taken up into the drama that is the being of God, we live by the blessed death of God. So this rationalist theology which is Hegel's philosophy unites the serenity of the Greeks with the profundity of Christianity. Misusing, at the least, the letter of the Gospels, it demands that the light of reason must not be dimmed by the death of God. Then the unhappy conscience will be cured of its unhappiness, the noble soul released from its pride and its separation, and man, reconciled with his acts, with the world and with history, will no longer need to delve into himself and question his own heart in order to become one with the divine whole in process of self-achievement. Transcendence, mystery and the interior life once despatched, man will enter upon knowledge of God, and God will know himself in man. The times will be accomplished.

We have only been able in the foregoing summary to distil the essence of Hegel's system, which one commentator has happily called "a pagan Christianity". The construction of this system is not achieved without some cheating. The Jewish mind and the Christian soul are capriciously tailored to fit the needs of a system which, while pretending to be completely rationalist, loses itself in the end, as we have just seen, in theosophy and illuminism. The young Hegel was distraught by an antisemitism of such violence that we sometimes suspect that a controversialist so ready to pile up his invective had a personal account to settle with Jehovah. The Christianity too, whose development Hegel described, was the Christianity of the

Reformation, which had already developed too far in the direction of individualist pietism and was already being swamped in the muddied tide of German Romanticism. But we must be careful not to slip into a too easy refutation which misses the point and does not face the essential problem. Hegel's "pagan Christianity", by challenging together the divine transcendence and the interior life of the soul, tried quite deliberately and with unequalled power to dechristianize not so much Christians as Christianity itself. So Hegelianism gave an impetus to all those, from Marx through Nietzsche to Sartre, who set about announcing the death of the Christian God. Contemporary atheism, so far as it has any common characteristic, is no more than a continuing echo of the case opened by Hegel against the "noble soul" and the "unhappy conscience".

True, the integrating Absolute of Hegel has not been popular in atheist circles. No one explicitly set himself up as Hegel's disciple. Many saw in his system yet another of the old theologies. But Marxism fell under the spell of Hegelianism for its humanity moving towards its fulfilment, deeply divided against itself by the class struggle, is singularly like Hegel's God, even to the point that it has to become completely unhuman in the proletariat in order to become fully human in the classless society. Atheist existentialists have no love for Hegel's philosophy, for they cannot but see in the hope of man's reconciliation with himself a mythological consolation, and therefore also resignation. Yet since Feuerbach no modern atheist, in accusing the Christian God of reducing men to slavery, has failed to take up the Hegelian ideas of master and slave, of the noble soul and of the unhappy conscience.

Contemporary atheism is, we said, a kind of humanism, because it claims to give back to man that part of himself transferred to God. A mind that recognizes in and above itself the enveloping mystery of God's sovereignty is thus disabled, weakened, deprived of its best part, the victim of a sort of self-mystification. So a man will only believe in God in proportion as he lacks the courage to be a man. These present-day atheist ideas derive directly from the case presented by Hegel against the unhappy conscience. And if we call this interior depth, proper to man, this restlessness which nothing finite can still, his soul, atheist criticism kills two birds with one stone and, Hegelian still in warring without respite against the unhappy conscience, under the pretext of setting men free, seeks both the death of the soul and the death of God.

But Hegel did not do what he set out to do. He claimed to be writing a fifth gospel, that of pure reason, substituting the God of the philosophers and the scientists for the God of Abraham, Isaac and Jacob, for the God felt in the heart. His intellectual descendants saw that he had abolished God and that the problem of God was less solved than done away with. They saw too that by using and changing the master's ideas it would be easy to reach the conclusion that at last, the heaven of man's imagining destroyed, man was free to exist. Feuerbach, the left-wing disciple, and Kierkegaard, Hegel's implacable opponent, both understood which way Hegelianism was moving: towards the decline of God and the rise of man. If we go back to the immediate origins of contemporary atheism we discover the genius of a rationalist reformer of the Christian faith, a reformer with no pity for the human heart, burning with irony against the justice of the prophets and the saints, and with a consuming passion for the absolute.

FROM MODERNISM TO ARCHAISM

There are, then, two kinds of answer to the question of the origins of contemporary atheism. First, atheism is a permanent possibility for man. Since God is not immediately evident, man and his condition in the world provide reasons, jumbled together and conflicting, for affirming and for denying his existence. The fact of atheism shows that a mental struggle is necessary to attain to knowledge of God's existence. Man is tempted to deduce the uselessness of God from the autonomy of human science, and the absence or impossibility of God from the evil man commits or suffers. The sources of atheism St Thomas uncovered can be seen in the contemporary mind; more actively pressing now, perhaps, than in other times, but substantially the same. Besides this, contemporary atheism would not be what it is if Hegel had not, by his phenomenology of the unhappy conscience, called into question the God of the Jews and of Christianity, in whom he saw only a feeble image of the real absolute. We do not claim to have demonstrated the actual influence of Hegel with proper historical strictness. For this we should have needed a great number of quotations and a massive erudition which would have been out of place here. Hegel's influence may have been indirect and have made itself felt gradually in the generations that followed him. An atheist like Comte, not given to deep speculations, remote from all, even Hegelian, metaphysics, could not have known Hegel; yet his thinking found for itself directions which can properly be called Hegelian. It is all exactly as if Hegel had been not merely an efficient cause but an exemplary cause, by erecting a lofty model, unchallenged by any rival, of a metaphysical argument in the grand manner which was intended to comprehend, to enfold, to pass beyond the Judaeo-Christian tradition. Some thinkers have aspired to this model, imitating it as far as they could, consciously or unconsciously; others follow its example whether they want to or not, because it is so pregnant with concentrated metaphysical thought. Even if Hegelianism did split up, which is both true and not true, even a splinter from this system, a spark struck off it, would be in itself a whole world of philosophy. The modern revolt against Christianity, with its concomitant political effects both on the right and on the left, owes its power and attraction in large measure to Hegel. If there is any originality in contemporary atheism it is Hegelian.

But, secondly, contemporary atheism has classical origins independently of Hegel. The attempt to overthrow God springs from a movement of the human mind which takes its outward shape, not its essence, from its own time, but which continually reiterates the same self-assurance of the intellect or the same anguish of the heart. By contrast, that atheism which is inspired by or grows out of Hegelianism has something romantic about it: for Hegel himself was profoundly influenced by that same German romanticism he claimed to destroy, but actually enabled to endure so much longer. This is in fact that romantic atheism which expands in an imposing poetry of existence, imagining that the stature of man increases as God descends into twilight; an atheism which calls itself new and in tune with the Faust-like spirit of the age, and calls upon modern man to put before everything else his own act of revolt; a progressive atheism which claims to wrest from a decadent and moribund Christianity the understanding and the direction of history.

But this modernism is illusory and artificial. This atheism, drunk with its progressiveness to the point of misunderstanding itself, was already constructed in antiquity: in Epicurus, for example, who relegated the gods to the ironic inactivity of the *intermundia*, the empty spaces between the worlds, and described a universe thus devoid of religion, brought into being by chance alone; for both these reasons, the removal of the gods and the chance origin of the universe, man was free, masterless, *adespotos*. Or, for example, in the myth of Prometheus, whom the young Marx claimed as the first atheist saint in his calendar; Prometheus, who snatched from the gods the secret of their power and invented a truly human civilization. Lastly, perhaps it is in the dawn of Greek philosophy, and especially in Heraclitus, so admired by Hegel and by Nietzsche, that we can find already, compressed and packed into the enigmatic beauty of brief fragments, the whole quintessence of this atheism which claims to be modern. The mysterious old aristocrat of Ephesus rejected transcendence and mystery and set contradiction between men and gods: "Immortals are mortal, mortals immortal: each lives in the death of the other, each dies the other's life."[13] Surely it is obvious that the fulness of God's being is made up from man's insufficiencies— his finitude, his dependence, his servitude—and that gods must die if man is to attain to such perfection as the laws of the cosmos allow him; that, in short, man and God are inversely proportionate one to the other? Before Christ and before Socrates, that anti-religious poetry which Hegel or Marx or Nietzsche was to take up and develop was already putting forth all its allurement without anything to do with either modern science or modern society. The so-called modernism of contemporary atheism is the oldest thing about it.

It is very significant, but not surprising, that men like Hegel and Nietzsche, more poets than scientists, were so insensitive to the scientific spirit and its development in a time of great discoveries and of important progress in the field of scientific knowledge. They were too full of memories of antiquity, too pre-Socratic, to be contemporaries of their own contemporaries in this regard. Besides, far from challenging the Christian God by arguing from the problem of evil, such men as Hegel and Nietzsche reduce the problem itself to nothing in an aesthetic vision of the world which is a revival and recollection of what was most ancient in Hellenism. This atheism which we have called romantic is thus alien to the most true and constant source of atheism's power, which St Thomas recognized and faced at the beginning of the *Summa Theologica*. Of the two components of contemporary atheism discerned and separated in this preliminary analysis, the one which appears most modern reduces to a retrograde archaism, and strives to dig up and rebuild "the deepest buried of all Greek temples", as Nietzsche said. On the other hand, that part of contemporary atheism which considers the power and scope of science, or which exaggerates and inflames that sensibility to evil proper to the heart of man, that is what is both most truly classical in it and most truly modern.

13 Heraclitus of Ephesus, fr. 62 (Diels).

This paradox is easy to understand after the first consideration of atheism. Hegel's "pagan Christianity" is not a real synthesis, giving birth to a new age, but resolves itself into a victory of paganism over Christianity, into an integration and assimilation of the antithesis into the thesis. What is most modern is lost, by a dialectic that is not Hegelian, in retrogression, and the vain attempt to pass beyond Christianity fails and falls back again into what is pre-Christian: a sign that Christianity is fundamentally unsurpassable. Our consideration of the proximate and ultimate origins of contemporary atheism has thus led us to a by no means insignificant doubt as to its real originality.

CHAPTER II

A HOUSE DIVIDED
AGAINST ITSELF

THE ROCK OF SISYPHUS

An atheist denies the existence of God; but he cannot deny the existence of the idea of God or of belief in God. These are psychological and historical facts, and enormous facts, of man's present as of his past. Such a denial is the less possible because atheism is a fighting creed which, in order to be itself, needs the assertion its denial so violently strikes out. Even if the idea of God is a morbid growth in the mind and belief in God a pathological phenomenon, in denouncing them as diseases atheism clearly presupposes their reality as diseases. Medicine cannot deny the existence of sick men who call it into being, nor can a cure repudiate the existence of the sickness which gives it purpose and meaning. To be able to cure a sickness intelligently, knowing what one is doing, one must know its causes. Atheism is thus only philosophically valid for man if it can reduce the idea of God to a dream, a myth, or a contradictory imagining, and if it can successfully psychoanalyse the religious consciousness. In fact, the idea of psychoanalysis, which now enjoys a considerable vogue, seems to have been developed before Freud as and when needed by aggressive antireligious thought. So it is not enough for atheism simply to declare that God is undiscoverable or impossible: it must find somewhere, on the earth or in man who is of the earth, the origin of the idea of God, and it must explain how man, simply as man, arrives at belief in God.

Besides, as Auguste Comte so soundly observed, only what is replaced is really destroyed. If for so many centuries and under so many climes men have hung their existence on something imaginary and irrational, then their misguided acts of faith, of piety and of adoration will only effectively be shown to be mistaken if they are preserved but applied to some object or value which is truly worthy of such a total effort of the heart and mind. Even a mystery religion has an individual and social function which, once religion is done away with, must be filled by a free-thinking system of knowledge or by rationalist politics. Supposing we admit all the destructive arguments of psychoanalysis, and grant that the idea of God is a bad dream or self-consolatory imagining of man which deludes his still slumbering mind; how can we explain this dream delusion without postulating some repressed and disguised desire which is thus relieved or symbolically and illusorily satisfied? When man awakes, the desire will presumably still be there: when atheism has shaken the sleeper, it must discover or invent an asceticism which will effectively destroy the desire, or a mysticism which will fulfil it. If it does not, nothing will have been achieved. If atheism's denial were to be taken to the extreme of nihilism, and claimed to destroy root and branch not only traditional religion but also its possible earthly, worldly substitutes, yet this nothingness put in the place of God, this emptiness produced by the removal of religious feeling, even if—indeed, especially if—they were to stay nothingness and emptiness, would produce in man a great anguish which this kind of atheism would find it difficult to describe or name or absorb into itself.

The fact of religious feeling is thus a challenge which atheism cannot refuse to take up. Marx and Comte, Nietzsche and Sartre, none has escaped facing this issue; all are compelled to explain belief in God and to replace it by a conceivable alternative world which is still habitable by man. Now to draw up a fair summary of contemporary atheism it is not enough to list these explanations and substitutes under a few simple headings as easily classifiable types. It is necessary to compare them with one another with some exactitude, and then we shall see that there are between them very lively disagreements and even brute contradictions. Neither on the psychoanalysis of religious feeling nor on the Being or Nothingness which arises when God is rejected does one atheist system agree with another. Hardly has one sort of atheism thought that it has done away with or destroyed God than it is faced by another sort of atheism even more dangerous to its principles and future than any religion or any theism. So it is forced to attack a substitute for God more intolerable than God himself, another vague illusion, another deceptive abstraction, and again unavoidably compelled to explain its origins in order to get rid of it. This is the labour of Sisyphus to which atheism is for ever condemned. The house it tries to build without God and against God is divided against itself.

The arguments advanced by atheism to explain the fact of religious belief actually produce contradictions. Sometimes the argument is based on the weakness of early man. At first, without sufficient scientific knowledge or technique, man created for himself fantastic images of nature and society: was he not dependent on both? How could he not feel, then, that he was surrounded by a mysterious power whose origin he could not see, which immeasurably outlasted his own fleeting existence, and which he had perforce to obey? So God is only nature or society, endured but not understood, a mythological construction bound up with an unawakened state of uncomprehended suffering. So, according to the dream-psychology proposed by Bergson and Alain, the world of dreams is reducible to the real world, but this reality is not penetrated, is blurred and confused and out of joint, because it is neither understood nor controlled. Sometimes, on the other hand, to explain away the assertion that there is a God, atheism invokes a mistaken intention to withdraw from and be independent of the world and of society: man thinks he is free because he is ignorant of the real physical and social causes which determine his existence. So say philosophers who oppose the idea of free will. Man imagines his freedom is complete, but it cannot in fact be fulfilled in this world. So, in his birth and death and in the brief time allotted to him man sees only the poor inverse of his being, the most wretched half, the true reality of which is an eternal idea in God, the true fulfilment of which is immortality in God. The dependence of man on society is the same dream-illusion as his dependence on nature. So God becomes the fallacy whose exposure justifies all insubordination; its fallaciousness is the revolutionary weapon used against all political order. By believing in God man is projecting into an anti-natural or anti-social heaven the false absolute of an illusory freedom.

There we have two explanations of the belief in God both leading to atheism but both radically contradicting one another. The first attributes man's having recourse to God to excess of collective humility, the second to unbounded individual pride. The one thinks of the believer as a man resigned, who must be awakened and set free from his fears and set on his own feet by the removal of God. The other claims to show that this same believer is a lawless anarchist who, by shattering his absolute freedom, must be taught obedience to the necessary and relative laws of nature and society. On the one hand the religious man is accused of bearing, without reacting into revolution, the weight of the world and the established constraints of society. On the other, the complaint is that he does not understand this world but runs away into a world of his own, that because of his longing for the absolute he cannot fully engage in the great enterprises of history, and that, in the end, unless he makes a great psychological effort, he is irrecoverably lost to rationally organized society.

Both these methods of refuting the idea of God are open to many variations, and they can be mixed together at the level of second-rate, incoherent propaganda. Nevertheless, they do spring from two contradictory philosophies, one clear in Marx or Proudhon, the other seen in Comte and Nietzsche. But the two kinds of accusation cannot be harmoniously used together in the same argument. It cannot at one and the same time be argued that God is that infinite weight of being which increases the natural heaviness of things to crush man utterly—in short, absolute positivity—and also that he is so transcendent that he becomes absolute negativity, emptying all reality of its substance and making the world a stage set with no depth, a shadow-theatre. By suggesting that God is unjustifiable, sometimes because he justifies everything, and sometimes because he justifies nothing, atheism confesses the fundamental duality of its own nature.

When it comes to replacing God and substituting another world for the religious one, atheism again proceeds to divide against itself and to split down the middle. One sort of atheism tries to suppress God and the divine completely, to get rid of— to speak the language of theology—God and his attributes together. It cannot admit that a shadow or reflection of God survives his death, for everything that is God or derived from God—the absolute, for example, or the holy—is considered as an obstacle in the way of the liberation of the whole man. There is another sort of atheism for which God is the symbol, provisional and ambiguous as all symbols are, of the kingdom of man that is to come or, more generally, of a truth immanent in the world to which mankind will come when it has outgrown the naïvety of its childhood and the abstract notions of its adolescence. For this sort of atheism, to replace God is precisely to realize his existence by destroying a transcendence and mystery which are only the mirages of the weakness and the ignorance of man. Then the world and man will be able to recover those attributes of God, reason and justice, which, potentially theirs, before the death of God were projected into an imaginary "beyond". Here again we find those two kinds of atheism, this duality which grows worse and worse until the contradiction is beyond healing.

In the first case, the removal of God reveals an unknown shore, where the random scattering of rocks and pebbles cannot make a world with sense and meaning. Epicurus' "chance" and the Existentialists' "absurdity" are good labels for this world that arose from none knows where, that exists without purpose, blind and indifferent, in which man, who knows that all the relationships he can establish, the bonds he can forge, are only accidents of chance meetings, nevertheless experiences the passionless exaltation or dejection of his independence or his forsakenness. It is all just as if God had made the world like a great poem, laden with hidden meaning, in which each word, rare or common, had been specially chosen and set in the unique position which should ever be its proper place. God once forgotten, the poem falls apart, relationships disappear, the once beautiful unity returns to its elements, and each word which once lived by its relations with others now knows only a solitary freedom.

In the second case, when God is taken away, the divine remains. For being is divine: as the cause of its own existence, it exists absolutely. Why should not the world, which the believer misrepresents in his longing for the "beyond", or humanity, which religion condemns to a perpetual tutelage, why should they not be divine, since they contain the cause of their own existence, to give them solidity and dignity? That omniscient and omnipresent Being, omnipotent and supremely just, who explains and justifies everything, and unceasingly radiates good and avenges evil, can we not see him now being actualized, thanks to the death of the God of transcendence and mystery, in the immanence of man's experience, at last clearly understood? According to the school of thought he is called Nature, Humanity or History. It is in him that man, reconciled with the earth and with time because of the collapse of the world "beyond", will find the courage to live and act, multiplying, growing stronger, strengthening the ties attaching him to the whole, to other men and the world, a whole now at last shining with its own light and no longer with that borrowed from an imaginary star.

The atheist is thus split in two, and the two kinds of world he struggles to build on the tomb of God are bound to contradict, to move apart from or even to destroy one another. Sisyphus imagines he has at last rolled his rock to the summit that will set him free: his labours are over, the fruits of victory are within his grasp. It is all an illusion! There is another hill, another slope as steep, the same wretched rock at the bottom and the same monotonous task to do again.

One atheist thinks he has achieved against God the final solidarity of mankind, and has gained by doing away with the great myth of God the adherence of man thus liberated to a world and a history now become rational. Against him stands the other sort of atheist, accusing him of being still under the spell of the God he pretends to deny; the fellow-atheist who is yet his enemy, who with all the resources of irony and critical exactness throws doubts on this too-well ordered world which moves with such wisdom towards the perfect realization of a great design. The Marxist boasts that he has understood and passed beyond Hegel, but there will always be an Existentialist to point out to him that he is really only a rather second-rate successor of the Bossuet of the *Discours sur l'Histoire universelle* or *La Politique tirée de l'Écriture Sainte*.

The other atheist is sure he has reached the limit of freedom, a freedom so much its own master in its aloneness that it shelters him, once God is abolished, from all authoritarianism and absolutism. And against him there stands the opposite kind of atheist, reproaching him with preserving in a rationalist and scientific age an attitude of withdrawal from the world, a hostility towards reality, obvious survivals from the ages of obscurantism. Only God could ever have excused such romanticism; too much enamoured of itself, it persistently refuses to find in the world or in history an object sufficient for the mind and satisfying to the heart. Has our atheist really rid himself of transcendence and mystery when we can see under the name of "absurdity" the reality of the irreducibly irrational, or when freedom is given the privileged meaning of absolute independence, with the result that man in the highest of his aspects does not really belong to the world at all?

So whichever choice the atheist makes, even if he has done his first task successfully and won his victory over God, all will have to be done over again, just as if nothing had been achieved. For his conquering atheism will have to combat another sort of atheism, itself also resplendent in all the glamour of modern enlightenment and fearlessness. This is a difficult situation: the evil that was God did not vanish when God vanished; the monster dead, the poison is still as virulently active, infecting atheism itself, making it fight again within itself the battle already fought against the enemy without. So the challenge of religion is not the only one atheism must face: it is fated to meet the equally rousing challenge of the other sort of atheism. It must always repeat all its labours, to show the origins of that other atheism and to refute its ideas, setting one world against another. In these controversies, so closely intertwined, are to be found not similar but the same critical arguments and destructive methods as were used against religion and now have to be brought into service again. One atheist now accuses the other of failing to exorcize the ghost of God, and of taking very good care not to throw away the core of man's religious inheritance. It is the labour of Sisyphus: the clumsy great rock is never rolled over the other side of hell into nothingness; and the greatest paradox is that it is atheism, divided against itself, which is both Sisyphus and the rock.

ATHEISM IS ARISTOCRATIC

Contemporary atheism provides numerous examples to demonstrate this internal opposition just described. The two princes of atheism, who by general consent are Nietzsche and Marx, had the same great ambition, not simply to do away with God by accumulating arguments but also to destroy for ever Christian civilization—which they both thought was in its death-throes—so as to substitute for it the values of a new culture of which each considered himself to be the prophet. Nothing illustrates the contradictions intrinsic in atheism better than the inevitable conflict between Nietzsche and Marx, who stand in the first rank of atheist thinkers. And if these princes of atheism were bound to be mutually incomprehensible even to the point of a battle between them which neither could ever atone for, yet each of them, having been bold enough to follow out his own intentions to the limit and accept all the consequences of his principles, found himself at the end in the basically tragic position of being quite unable to reconcile his results with his intentions or his conclusions with his principles. It seems that the fate of atheism is internal contradiction, that its inevitable sickness is antagonism between its two selves.

Nietzsche is incontestably highest in the atheist peerage. He snatched atheism away from the platitudes of scientists and positivists and with his astonishing creative power raised it to the height of great poetry. The famous saying of Robespierre, "Atheism is aristocratic", might have been said, not to justify the persecution of unorthodox intellectuals, but to render Nietzsche personal and particular homage before his time. So it may be fitting to break into these preliminary general considerations, without worrying about chronological order, in order to deal first with this prince of the strictest and at the same time, if we may so express it, the most luxuriant atheism.

Nietzsche was not a madman who claimed to have murdered God and was justly punished for this sacrilegious enormity by the mental breakdown of his last ten years. Apart from the fact that this is pagan reasoning, attributing to the true God the behaviour of the ancient Nemesis, to think thus is also seriously to misunderstand Nietzsche's thought itself. In fact, Nietzsche was sure that God was already dead, that believers and unbelievers alike knew very well that that dreadful event had already happened, that the crime of all crimes had been committed by each one as by all; but that each and all did their utmost not to admit what they had done and what they knew, because of the fear produced by the act and its consequences. It was not Freud, then, but Nietzsche who invented "repression". The corpse may be hidden, but it decomposes and infects the house. Nietzsche, over-sensitive to smells—all his genius, he said, was in his nostrils—broke the conspiracy of silence. Among all the murderers of God he was the one who let the secret out and cried it from the rooftops with the vehement indignation proper to the prophet; who shouted aloud what craven conformists hid in secrecy, in the darkest recesses of their conscious or unconscious minds.

God is dead; but was he ever living? Always, but according to Nietzsche especially since Platonism and Christianity conspired to turn the mind of man towards a beyond, God has only been the grandiose and empty image in which fear of life and hostility to reality found self-expression, concealment and justification. Here again Nietzsche anticipated Freud in psychoanalysing man. By stripping the mask from the myth he forced it to disclose the profound perversion of the instinct of life it thus pathologically represented. God is thus a symbol concealing man's powerlessness, which that very powerlessness produces, maintains, jealously preserves and defends against the light, so as to be able to continue in its not-being in peace in the shelter of that symbol.

Traditional theology says that God is eternal, immutable, simple; in him are the exemplary cause and also the creating principle of all things. But it was really the human mind itself, which forgot it was itself the first principle, and fashioned for itself this principle and creator, in paralysed abdication from its true creative powers. Because he has not the courage to stand up to the torrent of universal becoming, to the changeability which is the very rhythm of time and to the perpetual contradiction which life fully lived imposes on itself, man makes for himself this exemplarily unmoving truth in order to make lies of becoming, time and life. Eternity, immutability, simplicity—these are not positive ideas, with solid existence, self-consistent; they must rather be seen as negations inseparable from the faint heart which secretly makes them and attributes them to an absolute by a double self-deception. To posit a simple God is to flee from the bewildering complexity of the world; to posit an immutable God is to refuse to recognize that movement which is the breathing of the world, the very breath of its life; to posit an eternal God is to refuse to cast off on the deeps of time, to refuse to recognize, since all is already accomplished in God, the great adventure of the unforeseeable and the unknown. The denial of the world and of time is disguised as the affirmation of God.

The same traditional God, and especially the God of Jews and Christians, also has moral attributes. He is Justice and Love. In him and from him each man will receive his recompense, will obtain what he lacks, will be stripped of excessive riches; and this perfectly moral divine order, which will be clearly seen at the end of time or beyond time, is secretly and already realized in the mystery of the Kingdom. For Nietzsche, however, this God of ethics is the same product of resentment as the God of metaphysics, and there is nothing really positive in this Good which is taken to its limit; it is all negation of true values. Those men called to carry the passion of life to a violent extremity of joy or grief are only a small élite, few in number and profound in spirit. These brave fellows would never have invented God, for real aristocracies are Godless, or honour only gods of the earth, many gods, fleshly, warlike, like men's instincts themselves. But the weak, natures that are feminine and naturally inclined to suffer, victims who have resigned themselves to life's harshness, the multitudinous herd, envy their masters the possession of their powers, and still more the noble use of power, from all of which they themselves are forever cut off. To despoil their masters in an open fight is beyond their ability, besides which a straightforward defiance is contrary to their natural lack of spirit. All that is left to them is hypocritically to undervalue real power by making up a God for whom poverty becomes richness in spirit, weakness becomes a mysterious strength, defeat a means of access to an invisible power, affliction the way to a secret joy. God is merely the fictitious guarantee of a world of power turned topsy-turvy.

Such an invention has two advantages: first, the embittered, the angry and resentful, the defeated, parade in sham nobility and are convinced, according to a twisted Hegelian dialectic, that they are no longer slaves but have become the masters of their masters; and second, the few heroes whom the earth brings forth to join battle are not immune against treachery, as many legends show, and masters can be persuaded by the perfidious plausibility of slaves so as to doubt that their power is real or their values authentic. The idea, which comes from the herd, that they might have God against them, shakes their ancient security from within and they are infected by the masochistic sickness of the unhappy conscience; they lose heart, make the required sacrifice, and disown their nobility and their courage in favour of pity. When this happens, the morality of the herd rules universally among men, the world becomes Socratic, Jewish, Christian. The spirit of vengeance has carried it off, those who are truly alive are humbled, while those who are afraid to live are exalted by a trick. The slaves have won; God is shown to be an efficient weapon when it is a matter of bringing down the only true aristocracy of the earth. According to Nietzsche, then, God is in his moral as in his metaphysical attributes the expression, the symptom, the product of that mortal malady of the spirit which he calls nihilism, and which unnaturally prefers the peace of not-being to the fine flurry of life. God and nihilism are thus closely interconnected, the effect becoming in turn the cause of its own cause. There cannot be a greater mystification, for believing in God is precisely affirming that not-being is and being is not; or, and this is the same aberration, that powerlessness has power and power is powerless.

It is easier to understand this tragic capacity of negation to produce a fantastic image of itself called God, if one remembers that Nietzsche's universe, like that of Heraclitus, is one the essence of which is strife. Piously to pray for an end to all war, said the old aristocrat of Ephesus, is to pray for the end of everything: it is to profess nihilism, said Nietzsche, echoing the voice of ancient Greece. To believe in God, in a One, always the same, is to hold that the violent clash of opposites is damned and that all strife is fated to be lost in the depths of the divine peace. The drama that is the world loses its substance with its power and becomes a ridiculous farce. But the nihilist cannot escape the fate of all. This deserter from the battle is still a combatant, for to deny the strife is itself to join in the striving. So God is not Unity, Self-identity, Peace, secure above all strife, but the weapon used by the enemy of life to vilify and destroy life by reducing it to the condition of a mere appearance. God is not Justice or Love, who could confound all aggressiveness and heal every affliction; he is that best camouflaged but most deadly weapon which, in the great rebellion of the slaves, incurably wounds the strong and assures the victory of the herd.

This God, the standard of those who deny life, is the God of Socrates, the artificer of the decadence of Greece, whose *daimon* was even then the spirit who always says "No"; he is the God of the Jews, a people—for Nietzsche seems to be carrying on Hegel's anti-Semitism—politically incapable and for ever wandering in exile, and hence doomed to resent the beauty of this world and the glory of empire; he is the God of the Gospels, of the *Magnificat* and the Sermon on the Mount, whose disciples are asked to worship as divine precisely what is most opposed to life. In God, therefore, absolute denial triumphs, and it is in a tragic world, in a tragic apotheosis of death, that Nietzsche discovers, with a mixture of terror and exaltation, the truth of God.

Thus to announce the death of God is to prophesy to man, or at least to the elect who are mankind's highest representatives, the hope of victory over death. All the abundance of invective and parable that fills the last works of Nietzsche surely sprang from a burning certainty that may be called religious: the death

of God is the death of death. The two great elements of Nietzsche's thought, or rather, of his vision, the superman and the
eternal return, only have meaning through this desire to find
in a wholly atheist creed a religion of complete salvation for
the world and man. The eternal return is the world when it is
saved; the superman is both the saviour and the saved. There
is the conclusion of Nietzsche's logic; and there too emerges
the contradiction between the original vision of Zarathustra
and the *ultima verba* of his message.

God is dead, he who made the earth only a dim reflection of
the only Being worthy of the name, and the earth henceforth
exists alone and wholly, exists with a full and bounding life:
how could it perish, since death is dead? That eternity which in
God is only a gloomy negation becomes the active and joyful
attribute of a world with neither beginning nor end, which never
falls below its own greatness. So by bathing in the glory of
eternity all that is and lives in the world comes fully to exist.
But how can the finite and transitory things of this world both
pass away and not pass away? How can they die and not die?
How can they be saved, except by the eternal return of all
things, because of which we know that what has once deserved
to exist will return as it was, as it is, and as it shall be? So the
centre is everywhere, the present is eternal and "once"
means "for ever", for the gift of existence cannot be taken
away, the world never goes back on itself.

The God of pity and charity is dead, because we now know
that by lending his authority to the frailty of the weak and by
destroying the might of the strong he threw a shadow of death
over every enterprise productive of real values and real power.
The weak who dispute true authority, who reproach Caesar for
being Caesar, do not live and act in this world: they are content
to offset their submission with the ideal rewards of conscience
and the imagined compensations of the life beyond. If to live
is to create, the weak are living dead, and the strong, shackled
and insulted, insidiously tyrannized and tempted to become
tyrants, never attain to the fullness of life. The superman of

tomorrow cannot yet be described, for he presupposes a profound change in man. So Nietzsche never spoke of the superman except as the prophets spoke of the saviour to come, in veiled predictions, more full of warmth than light, which only the actual coming can make truly understandable. But Nietzsche was inspired to believe, or convinced himself, that in this saviour's putting forth his strength there would be generosity and love: the superman would have "the head and shoulders of a bull and the face of an angel". In the time when there was a God, man lost himself seeking strength in the denial of power. When man is saved, the superman will live the full life, and by uniting for the first time the love of power and the power of love he will be invincible, in that imperishable world, against the temptations of death.

Must the death of God mean that the old mythologies will be reborn? This superman and eternal return are indeed echoes of ancient ideas. The superman is not new: he is a sort of reincarnation of the hero of legend, alone between gods and men, killer of monsters, half-god, half-man, who suffers indescribably but triumphs on the pyre of his apotheosis, and whose strength, wholly to be seen in this world, is the pattern, like that of Hercules, of all strength. The eternal return goes back to the same mythological ancestry: other lovers of fate, such as Heraclitus and the Stoics, made it into a doctrine of their system to justify or to symbolize in a satisfying way their faith in the divinity of the world. Before them, poets had begotten the idea and, making even then a religion of irreligion, had set the ephemeral in an eternity visible to the eyes and sensible to the heart. It is surely an indisputable rule that an anti-Christian is simply a pre-Christian.

Nietzsche wagered that the new man, who would soon dare to make this world his only law, would save both himself and the world: a wager made in the nineteenth century and lost in the twentieth, as we shall see in the chapter on politics. What is more, this vision of the superman and the eternal return, intrinsically so essential to Nietzsche's atheism, is also the greatest test of him as a prophet: it concerns the beginnings, the foundations of his thought. How is a superman, who is to be a living synthesis of opposites, possible in a world of antagonism and partiality? How can we understand that he might bring both peace and war? Does he stand on the height to fulfil or to condemn the world? Does he not remain, like the Christian saviour, an enigmatic contradiction? But, in a world in which strife and violence have been glorified beyond measure, he could easily be, as Nietzsche himself saw with some anxiety, the type of some unheard-of tyranny to come. Instead of the myth of the eternal return giving substance, life and meaning to the world, does it not reduce it to the most senseless of appearances? If everything begins again and yet nothing begins, there is neither present nor future, and the past has consumed, without leaving a morsel, the whole of time. How can an eternity be made from a time so destroyed and devoured? The course of the world becomes inevitably fated, with neither pity nor pardon; this earth men so desperately wanted to live is as dead as death itself, and man or superman, compelled to live over and over again an existence already accomplished, are not real beings but shadow-characters. Everything Nietzsche rejected with horror—the eternity of death, the winter-sleep of life, existence as it were frozen in ice—all this he himself recreated with his artistry and with his prophetic inspiration, so that the dungeon merely became deeper and smaller, and in the end the face of terror was seen with a kind of holy dread beneath the mask of joy.

Stripping the dead God of his attributes as one might spoil a corpse, and giving them back to men and the earth, changes the freedom that should have been complete into an equally total servitude. Like Hegel, Nietzsche tried to make the ideas of God and of salvation completely pagan. Hence the intolerable contradictions which ultimately arise. As befits a leader, this prince of atheism gathered together the whole essence and destiny of the enterprise. He is Sisyphus and the rock, he is the house divided against itself. In the last analysis, the superman and the eternal return are only symbols to express and to gloss over the contradiction of a pagan Christianity in which the world is God and the superman is the Saviour. It is bitter-sweet to contemplate this impossibly beautiful idea so as to divert and to appease one's anguish—or to seem to do so—but if by some black magic it were to become a reality, flesh and blood, then it would change men into the damned and earth into hell.

PROMETHEUS THE SAVIOUR OF MANKIND

Marx and Marxism present us with quite a different world. In place of the aristocratic opponent of the herd only arguing with any feeling with superior men like himself, as though with his brothers, we have a tribune of the plebs, a plebs quite without a name, the multitude of the oppressed and the exploited. In place of poetry leaping from peak to peak we have an involved and laborious prose where sparks only gleam forth because they are so rare. It looks—but only looks—as though Marx was only worried about the problem of God for a brief moment at the beginning, whilst Nietzsche was obsessed by it throughout his work. But how different, how opposed to one another are the views each took of their common enemy! For Marx, God is the metaphysical bogey-man, long powerful but soon to be ineffectual, with which the privileged classes kept mankind, alienated from both man's true spiritual and his true temporal nature, in ignorant obedience. Against this, as we have just seen, Nietzsche thought of God as the weapon, both of attack and defence, used by the most effective leaders of the slaves against the thrones, principalities and powers of this world. On the one hand atheism is to set the slaves free from the tyranny of their masters, on the other, the superman from the shackles of the herd. Marxism may explain many things in history, but not how a Nietzsche could arise as a preacher of atheism. Nietzsche could make room for Marx or the Marxists neither among the supermen of atheism nor among the resentful crowd whose imaginary prop he held God to be. So when a Nietzschean (if there can be Nietzscheans who do not in some way falsify Nietzsche) calls a Marxist a barbarian opposed to all culture, and when a Marxist describes Nietzsche's thought as the raving of violent pride, these intolerant caricatures are not to be explained merely as due to the intellectual weakness of the controversialists. At bottom there is a brute contradiction and antagonism which cannot be resolved. A dialectic of opposition and division is thus recognizable in its products. Nietzsche intended the death of God to bring to man "the gift of perfect solitude"; for Marx, the final forgetting of God was to be the sign that men had attained to perfect solidarity. We have seen, and we have shown, that the atheist prophet of solitude and the atheist prophet of solidarity are necessarily cut off from mutual understanding. Atheism cannot do justice to all its forms; but a Christian philosophy in the tradition of Pascal can do so.

Atheism is the first principle and seminal reason of Marxism. Everything follows from it, and everything points back to it. An agnostic who refuses to deny the existence of God as firmly as he refuses to affirm it, but holds to an "I don't know", can no more make a real Marxist than a believer. Man's self-consciousness, the knowledge man has of himself according to Marx, cuts out completely the very possibility of a God, so that faith can only be a function of man's ignorance of himself. The whole being of man is in action, in work, by which man ceases to be an animal naturally adapted to nature, and adapts nature to himself by changing it, creating his own conditions for existence, thereby creating also himself. In short, the life of the worker does not presuppose but precisely makes and is one with the essence of man. Work therefore takes away from nature all authority over man, and if it is properly understood and fully experienced it constitutes an empirical proof of the non-existence of God, for a worker is origin, principle and cause of himself and of everything human in the world. Marxism is a revolutionary creed, for in the beginning is the revolution: that is, work, which forms the basis of man's condition by tearing him free, suddenly, by revolution, with a violent break, from the accidents of nature and the mysteries of the supernatural. Such is the meaning of that myth Marx quotes in his earliest works, the story of Prometheus, the Titan who spurned the gods and saved mankind by discovering all the arts and crafts.

Work itself is thus a creative and liberating force for man, but to realize itself fully it must suffer patiently for a long time, for that long time we call history. The oppressive restraints put on work by a society in turn based on slavery, feudalism and capitalism, run clean contrary to the essential nature of work by making the Promethean act itself dependent and servile, so long as men must work for the few among them who have property and power. Men then fall into misery, for whoever enchains work enchains men. This is the state Marxism was to describe by a famous term which derived from Hegel, alienation, in which was seen the origin of religion. God is born of a violence done to work, and therefore of an outrage against man. Man enslaved, alienated from himself, deprived of what is most human, possessing only his biological existence, creates for himself a symbolic compensation, and wanders from his proper path into an ideal and futile revolt, creating a Somewhere-else, making a religion and a God for himself. So he justifies and strengthens his established oppressors. "Religious misery", said Marx in a famous passage,[1] "is on the one hand the expression of real misery, but on the other it is a protest against real misery. Religion is the sigh of man oppressed, it is the soul of a world with no heart, as it is the spirit of a time with no spirit; it is the opium of the people." Marx here shows himself an apt pupil of Hegel,[2] that violent

---

[1] *Contribution to the Criticism of Hegel's Philosophy of Law.*

[2] Explaining in characteristic fashion, violently anti-Roman and anti-Christian together, how the first disciples of Christ converted a whole world, the young Hegel wrote: "Thus the despotism of the Roman emperors had chased the human spirit from the earth and spread a misery which compelled men to seek and expect happiness in heaven; robbed of

exponent of the unhappy conscience, from whom he sought keys to open all doors, borrowing both the explanation of the worse and the hope for the better. The whole of Marxism really stems out of the Hegelian master-slave dialectic. Work—and this is Hegel, letter and spirit—which was the testing experience of a fall, is to become the means of redemption. The worker-slave is the efficient agent of history who is to bring the great adventure to its close, who is destined to become the master of his master, to do away completely with domination as well as servitude, to restore labour to its pristine and fundamental truth, and in the same act to remove God by removing the social conditions which made that great mystification possible. Marxist political theory is thus lit through and through by the idea, not without its greatness, that Marx had of man and of labour. It is therefore atheist in its principles as in its final result, which is the establishment of a world of man no longer in any way alienated; that is, a world without God, a humanity like a collective Prometheus, conqueror of Zeus and only master of himself and the world.

Philosophically, then, Marxism is an atheist interpretation of Hegel. Historical materialism did not come from a sociological or scientific inquiry: the theory of the class struggle expresses in the prose of history the poetic idea of the universal struggle of master and slave. Marx's materialism properly so called is not the product of reflection on the natural sciences, it has nothing scientific or positivist about it, but is only the rudely polemical name given to a substantially Hegelian atheism. The "matter" of the Marxists is not the matter that modern physics has stripped of spirit or secret potencies; nor is it (and this ignores something of Prometheus' message) the

---

freedom, their spirit, their eternal and absolute element, was forced to take flight to the deity. The doctrine of God's objectivity is a counterpart to the corruption and slavery of man." "The Positivity of the Christian Religion", trans. T. M. Knox; in Hegel, *Early Theological Writings*, with an Introduction and Fragments translated by Richard Kroner; Univ. of Chicago Press, 1948, p. 162.

object and the means of human labour. It is confused with universal being, reality, what is given but is, if we may put it thus, its own giver, possessing in itself the cause of its own existence and of all its changes; for, following Hegel's teaching, nothing moves in history or in nature except by virtue of the contradiction that sets each thing against itself. The identification of matter with being in this way means nothing other than a complete immanentism that precludes any transcendence. Being is godless, being is matter: the phrases are strictly equivalent. Such materialism is rightly called dialectical; and Marx found this key to the universe, like the others, in the pocket of Hegel.

The theory is too close to the poetic sublimity of Hegel to lack all greatness, but it involves some inconsistencies. Even if Marx mutilates man by identifying his being with the act of labour, he sees clearly that although man is wholly rooted in nature he nevertheless surpasses it in his labour by reducing it to the status of an object and by producing clear proof of his own freedom. This is a Promethean proof of the emergence or transcendence of man, which is also a sufficient refutation of dialectical materialism. For that theory goes back to a pre-scientific and pre-Christian idea of the world as an animated or divine being, as an eternal power having in itself the principle of its own metamorphoses, of which man can only be the product and image. Such a Promethean theory of labour is a form of humanism, for it distinguishes and opposes spiritual freedom and inanimate things. Dialectical materialism is a kind of hylozoism which, in the ancient tradition, confuses spirit and matter. The choice has to be made between these two.

According to Marx, the critique of religion must end in the doctrine that man is the supreme being for man. But the whole man who grows with history and gives history its meaning is not the one who passes so swiftly and seeks the meaning of the history of which he sees himself so small a part. He is the incarnation of Hegel's absolute, and he betrays his origins. So atheism becomes pantheism. And this God is not incapable of reducing to slavery those who, whether they like it or not, are the steps to his actualization, the means to his self-achievement. The man who makes humanity bring into being the supreme being may perhaps provide himself with a harsher master than the masters of history—history itself. Historical materialism is no more a kind of humanism than dialectical materialism, since in not allowing the emergence of man and providing no basis for the worth of man as a free person, it makes man the slave of a myth or of an abstraction.

Marx, like Nietzsche, who is Eteocles to his Polynices, is a disciple of that paganization of Christianity of which Hegel provided the most powerful, unrivalled exposition. The eternal return and the superman, and the dialectics of progress and of Prometheus the liberator, these make two worlds challenging, provoking, scandalizing each other; yet in both can be seen quite plainly less a radical denial than a pagan transposition of Christianity. Eternal return or invincible progress in history, both are God descended into time, confounded with time, and giving all things consistent meaning. Superman or Prometheus the liberator, these are the saviour appointed by the inspiration of the world or by the pressure of history to set man free from a certain limit of misery called nihilism or alienation. The Christian God, for Nietzsche as for Marx, is only a slave's dream which makes a religion of his slavery; but their atheism does away with neither God nor salvation, it merely sets one God against another, one salvation against another.

THE DEVIL'S KITCHEN

Nietzsche and Marx represent the twin peaks of nineteenth-century atheism. From their time to our own atheism has spread and proliferated, at times popular and simplified, at others aristocratic and refined. Marxism, the practical success of which is one of the most important events of the century, has become an atheist religion dragging up in its propaganda the old arguments of a naïve and platitudinous scientific positivism. We shall return to this in the chapter on political theory. The surrealists tried to make art and poetry of atheism, and over and beyond their excesses, their esotericism, their sacrilegious parodies, they sometimes achieved a Satanic heroism which made one tremble. Besides these things, whenever in philosophy or literature rationalism makes the denial of transcendence or the removal of mystery the condition of thought, if not the actual task of thinking, then a step is inevitably taken towards atheism, though that atheism is sometimes anonymous and unrecognized. If Valéry or Alain were unwilling to label themselves atheists, this was only for social or political reasons, and their fastidiousness really altered nothing. But it is in atheist existentialism, and the name may be more than simply a convenient label, that atheism has been carried to a degree of virulence—and also of strict purity—which seems new in its history. There is now an attempt to uproot and destroy not only God but the very ideas of religion and salvation.

Such is certainly the intention or, to use his own terminology, the fundamental project, of Sartre: God is impossible. Everyone knows this, but refuses to admit it for fear of being forced to assume the burden of absolute freedom. The faith of believers is therefore only dishonesty, bad faith. But outside religion there is no salvation. Whatever the risks of his condition, man is forced to face the fact of his existence. This series of closely connected propositions sums up the whole philosophy of *Being and Nothingness*. Metaphysician, novelist and dramatist, Jean-Paul Sartre professes his atheism with an easy assurance backed, in philosophy, by an extraordinary academic virtuosity bristling nevertheless, not only in dramatic dialogues but also in technical treatises, with a polemical vigour which reminds us of the surrealists in making contemptible Aunt Sallys of his adversaries. Sartre's originality lies in his aggressively learned manner, in his prodigious verbal felicity, and in his unique ability which is, however, quite unpoetic, to give abstractions an almost tangible solidity. His matter is most commonly borrowed from others. As the heir of an already established tradition of atheism, Sartre has undertaken to cleanse it of any religious survivals it has carried along with it, and so to inflame to action systems which until he came along were timid and hesitant: his only task is to strip them of their innocence. The ingredients Sartre throws into his pot come from other people, but at least he knows how to make them boil merrily.

Sartre's philosophy is sometimes taken for a French version of German phenomenology and existentialism, and the author of *Being and Nothingness*, who thanked Husserl for having saved him from the Sorbonne, is in a way the French Heidegger. Heidegger's thought is essentially a rediscovery and deepening of the sense of the finiteness and contingence of all existence. Hence the ideas of abandonment and of nothingness which have an atheist flavour. The limit which makes things finite is really that absolute horizon which inflexibly surrounds existence and so gives it unity and solidity, that is, actuality. From this the conclusion may be drawn, by a sort of inverted ontological argument, that there can only be finite existence and infinitude is therefore a chimera. Resolute fear, or anguish (*Angst*) before death is the *amor fati*, inflexible adhesion to a destined finitude. Beyond the finite there is nothing, and our enlightenment is only precious, our noisy confusion only pitiable, against the background of that silence and that darkness. Heidegger's idea of man, the "sentinel of nothingness", is really the same as Sartre's. It is true that in these last few years Heidegger's philosophy has developed and changed, and man's existence is now the door opening on a Being which is indescribable, imperceptible, but omnipresent and all-enveloping. The "sentinel of nothingness" has become "the shepherd of Being". Heidegger's opponents, who are mostly to be found among the Marxists, have been able to insinuate somewhat wickedly that the master has two philosophies, one for a time of unrest and war, the other better adapted to periods of peace, and that this accounts for the shift from a military to a bucolic metaphor, the sentinel becoming a shepherd and nothingness being softened and changed into Being. Whatever may be the truth of this historical question, it would be wrong to rank Heidegger with the atheist existentialists. Whatever shape his philosophy takes, it precludes all knowledge of God of a metaphysical or theological kind, but at the same time, in spite of first appearances, it does not declare itself either for or against the existence of God. Heidegger's nothingness remains equivocal, and could be a way of not committing oneself, of protecting mystery against mistaken conceptualization or deceptive symbolization. Heidegger was right to deny any suspicion of paternal responsibility for Sartre's philosophy; whatever correspondences there are between the two systems are not of the kind which betokens influence of one on the other.

The real origins of Sartre's atheism lie rather in his years of apprenticeship, when his masters were Alain rather than Husserl, Valéry and even Brunschvicg rather than Heidegger. Sartre identifies consciousness with Nothingness (*le Néant*), which does not mean that mind is nothing and materialism true. By Sartre's Nothingness must be understood, not Heidegger's *das Nichts*, but that power to make a denial which is the mind itself; a power which the mind, whatever it does, exercises unceasingly once it is awakened and no longer confounded with what Valéry called the "tangible emptiness" of the body and the physical world. "To think is to say, No"; "The mind is the denial of the object": one maxim is Alain's, the other academic idealism's. They are the harmless elements of a chemistry which Sartre turned into an alarming alchemy by putting forward the same doctrines in the shape of an impious philosophy of mind. Sartre's existentialism is the philosophy of the old Sorbonne carried off by force to the witches' sabbath. Since to doubt and to deny, so we are told, are the highest acts of man, to believe or to affirm must be to fall from full humanity, to enter an animal sleep, "to behave like oysters", as Valéry said. But such behaviour is a lower limit which it is in fact impossible to reach, for the mind, which is essentially negation, cannot be conscious of believing except by separating itself from its belief, by holding it at a distance, by denyi ng it. So we can see the value and the implications of the statement we have already met, according to which all faith is bad faith. It is this that justifies Sartre's scorn for others.

So the departure of God is arranged with cheerful sophistry: first, because belief as such is folly, and second, because even if, *per impossibile*, God existed, man could do no other than deny him, by hurling himself away and beyond, emptiness drawn to emptiness. Faust, because he put first the free act of will, is inseparable from Mephistopheles, "the spirit who always says, No". A created free will would be a living contradiction of its creator, as Sartre wished to imply in *The Flies*. There as elsewhere, anti-theism is a symbolic mythology of atheism. A free creature is the same sort of contradiction as a square circle. A consciousness both free and created and kept in being by its creator, would be neither conscious nor free. God and freedom cannot exist together without one destroying the other.

Freedom is thus a sufficient proof that there is no God; the idea is not new. But it remains to show how the illusion that God exists is possible. It is so, according to Sartre, because man and the world suffer the same incurable division; God is thus that unity which is bound to be postulated, but postulated in vain.

There is a cleavage in "human reality", to use Sartre's deliberately shocking anti-personalist expression. Since man is free he is other than his being; that is, other than his body, and other also than that other body made up of his opinions and feelings, which are for ever changing. The true me, the sum of my determinants, is known or knowable by others, but inasmuch as I am a free mind I am the negation of my own reality, I challenge my true self. I think, therefore I am not what I am (the good old *cogito* is also pressed in for the witches' sabbath of Nothingness). I escape myself, I flee before myself, less expecting a clear future than moving towards nothing and nowhere. In short, I am "pro-jected", for so is an innocent word split up to make it say more than it can or should. Condemned to be free, that is, condemned to this perpetual exodus, man thus lives in the anguish of always losing himself and never being able to rejoin his other self. Hence there naturally arises his desire to be equal to himself, to have a soul as representable, as determinate, and as substantial as the body, to fill the nothingness of his freedom with the plenitude of being, to halt this meaningless flight and bring peace. To meet myself, to know my own soul, would be to find God, who is really that being by virtue of which I can reconcile myself to myself. But to do away with the cleavage which makes me myself would be the suicide of my free consciousness. God is the same thing as death.

Moreover, the mind is bound to be in the world, since in some inexplicable way it comes out of it: like a squash ball it needs the solid wall of the world to deny it, to rebound into emptiness and so prove its elasticity. But this same mind is not truly of the world, for the aerial lightness of the "for itself" is an explosion of nothingness in the heavy mass of the "in itself". Now God is merely the imaginary cure of the incurable cleavage. He is an illusion, but a necessary one which cannot make the passage from the ideal to the actual, because the unity of this duality, agreement between mind and matter, means the victory of matter over mind and the burying of a world now without light in the dense night of existence. Once again, God is the same thing as death.

So man and the world cast behind them the shadow of God. He is as it were the imaginary scar of a wound which is still, as the mind well knows, open and festering. Here metaphysics becomes ethics. Man's existence, haunted by this obsession, this longing for an impossible fulfilment, is utterly frustrated and can only remain true to itself, really worthy of being lived, by refusing to believe, as it is continually tempted to believe, in God and in salvation. This is a turning upside-down of the world of religion carried to a frightening degree. What has meaning and value cannot exist, what exists is for ever meaningless; the longing for God is unpardonable, and there is no salvation except in the despairing renouncement of all salvation. A Christian is bound to find himself thinking that a philosophy so cunningly constructed to dishonour and destroy all faith and all wisdom must have been cooked up in the devil's kitchen.

But Sartre invented very little. His "in itself" and "for itself" lead to other thinkers who have become respectably and even honourably established. Alain's "naked existence", which neither loves nor hates, which can neither approve good nor reprove evil, which never says yes or no, and consequently leaves man an entirely free choice for which he alone is responsible; this anticipates Sartre's "in itself". The writer of *Nausea* had only to change the style of its description, giving an indefinable air of smuttiness to this superfluous being, which absurdly and indecently exists, as unfeeling as a stone. A freedom which creates ideal values is a characteristic notion of idealist philosophy, and it is a commonplace of the schools that no value can be actualized without denying itself as a value; it is no great novelty, whatever Sartre may say, to talk of man as a free existent creating his own essence. Sartre's originality lies entirely in his methods, and consists in his having deliberately forced an atheist meaning on to ideas already current, ideas which seemed benevolently neutral, such as the opposition between idea and reality: if this is made an absolute antagonism it inevitably leads to the impossibility of God. Sartre's own contribution is one of style and feeling. So, for example, human freedom, although it invents in its solitude values for which it assumes the whole responsibility, yet has something of divinity about it; but in Sartre the same freedom, also solitary and equally responsible for values only having meaning for itself, has to fold its wings, being given over to a precarious changeability, and described as empty of

being and of divinity. Spirit, which was for idealists the glory of
the universe, is in Sartre a shameful disease. It is always the
same method, turning things upside-down: turn the picture
back again, and it is recognizable enough.

In Sartre too is that echo of Hegel which is the fate of all
atheism: the theory of the unhappy conscience, and the master-
slave dialectic, both used here against God.

Religious consciousness mystifies itself when it allows itself
to believe that its anguish can be ended by its losing its freedom
in the perfect being. So, as in Hegel, an objective and transcendent God is the illusion of the unhappy conscience. But, as
opposed to Hegel, when the illusion is dispelled, the unhappy
conscience remains the unhappy conscience, with no other
course open to it than sternly to brace itself to bear its un-
alterable state of unhappiness.

The master-slave dialectic, which Sartre seems to make the
permanent and unchangeable truth of human relations, blows
like a constant wind on the sails of atheism's mills. Man is
the enemy of man, for strictly Hegelian reasons. The plurality
of intelligent beings is scandalous, for there ought only to be
one spirit, and Hegel went so far as to postulate a descent of
the Absolute in order to explain the inexplicable. When Sartre
removes the divine Absolute, the scandal remains. There is
something intolerable about the presence in the world of
anyone else: it dispossesses me, steals my freedom from me.
For, being free and unceasingly projected ahead of myself,
I do not live, I only play at living, acting out the farce of my
own life, which is only real in the countless glances directed
at me by others. So at one and the same time we are to one
another slaves, since what we have of objective reality is
granted us by others, and masters, both because we pay them
for the parts they play and because our inviolable freedom
escapes out of the clutches of others into its perpetual flight to
somewhere else. Love, which is a concordance or fusion of
freedoms, is thus the same sort of illusion as God or salvation.
To love is to choose to be either dominant or dominated, or

each in turn. Far from reconciling me to myself, the presence of others most cruelly forces me to see the dichotomy of my own state, and contributes another proof of God's maleficence, if he existed. For what is God but an absolute Other who, far from ending the master-slave dialectic, carries it to an extreme point of exacerbation? For if others are hateful, God must be absolutely hateful. Atheism sometimes seems mournfully to regret having so utterly refuted a God who, if he existed, would provide man with opportunities for such noble rebellion. So it has to raise the dust of a fictitious battle with an imaginary God; and yet the comedy has in it an element of tragedy.

The world of atheism is now perfectly ordered. It lacks nothing, for it has become the kingdom of nothingness. Over its gate is fixed an inscription mocking at "filthy hope". It is all on view, with nothing hidden, for those thrown together to form the innumerable populace are empty within, all their truth being entirely public in that intercourse of word and action which makes an uninterrupted hubbub. They are not indifferent to one another but bound by ties of passion, because for each one the existence of someone else is both necessary and unbearable. Bodies and souls are mingled and mixed without shame, while individual freedoms are so lost in bewildering flight that no one is neighbour to anyone else. No one can reach agreement, can give a blessing, can say "amen", except by inventing a sort of show, a petty distraction, which by no means fools the public entertainer who cooks it up. Clarity becomes a curse: and since in this city of scattered and discordant elements there is no king above or supreme judge to curse, the curse falls back on itself and burns in its own fire. But peace and happiness, God and salvation, which everyone knows to be falsehoods, are still so tempting that the less cowardly stiffen their courage by ceaselessly and blasphemously refuting the impossible Being whose essence surrounds non-existence. Their invectives against the Absolute as blind, deaf and dumb as matter itself, or against the infinite

Spirit, are like a shameless and killing glance that strips and
kills all that it lights upon. But sacrilege is a sham, passion
futile, in a world of torture without a torturer, of exile without
a homeland. It is as if the product of the devil's kitchen is hell
itself.

THE DISPROPORTION BETWEEN ATHEIST SYSTEMS

The three systems which have just been analysed—and this
analysis frees us from any necessity to examine minor variants
—show clearly enough that atheism is bound to produce
contradictions. The battle between these systems, which is
a conflict of atheism within itself, has actually taken place and
will always take place. Sartre may very prudently have made
himself the enemy of all enemies of Communism; he may have
suggested, insidiously and circumspectly, that Marxism needed
to be "completed in its subjective aspect"; he may have seen
a good weapon in dialectical materialism, a myth useful for
the time being in the class struggle of the proletariat. But
his reference to the limits of Marxism and his attempt to justify
it in a modernist and pragmatic way have been resented by
thorough-going Communists, and from one end to the other
of the Communist world existentialism has had many brickbats
thrown at it, being accused of obscurantism and of being the
product of a bourgeois world in decay.

This is because Sartre discovered in the denial of God a
human freedom which is total, without chart or compass or
star to guide, while Marxists see in it humanity marching with
sure step towards ends already determined in human nature
and fully realizable by man's own Promethean powers. On one
side we have an individual and individualist free will so absolutely free that all idea of liberation is called mystifying or
mythological; on the other, a hope for collective liberation, a
hope of such fullness that there is no salvation other than
adherence to the necessity of history, so that free will becomes

a fictitious abstraction. Comte and Marx were setting forth an atheism at once surpassed and made actual: humanity was the Being which, like God, contained within itself the reason for its own existence, and was the identification of power with value, power such that there could be no greater, value such that there could be no higher. This God of positivism was to explain and justify the course of the world's history, to give to knowledge its highest rule and to action its determining criterion. Sartre makes the denial of God the true act of the mind. For him, atheism cannot be surpassed. The idea of God is constantly and unremittingly the opponent of thought, which puts itself to the test by not yielding; so much so that this missing, impossible God gives to Sartre's world a sort of infernal dimension. So atheism, of whatever kind, cannot entirely leave behind the idea of God. It lives on this capital. Either it realizes God in this world in nature or in history, or it declares him impossible to find in this world and contradictory in himself. Whatever strength it has, whether it is positive or negative, atheism has it from the idea of God. Whatever weakness it has derives from the use it makes of that idea.

It is now time to break this symmetrical antithesis, setting one against another the atheism of solidarity, of Comte or Marx, and the atheism of solitude, of Nietzsche or Sartre, and to set out the disproportion between them. The first, which tries to realize God, has a political purpose. As we can see in Comte and Marx, it intends to remake society from top to bottom and to give man the full mastery of the world. But its historical dynamism is compensated by its great intellectual and spiritual weakness. It is always quite incapable of taking up the challenge to itself constituted both by Christianity and by the other form of atheism, which despairs completely of God, and which can be called true or integral atheism.

Metaphysically, political atheism reduces to pantheism; it revives the ancient paganism and gives a modern scientific appearance to the old idols of the soul of the world and the genius of history. In so far as it is properly political, this form of atheism will be expressed in a totalitarian system which makes spiritual freedom a nonsensical impiety. For Christianity to defeat such atheism it is enough that it understands it and makes it see that it has only proclaimed the death of God in order to replace it too hastily by the great god Pan and the deified Caesar. The arguments of integral atheism, too, are irrefutably effective in their mockery and destruction of these new but very ancient gods of nature and history. All their shots, even where they think to aim against the Christian God, score a bull on this target.

Integral atheism seeks and claims to have found a decisive proof against God in the order, or rather the absence of order, of this world. It sees discord and contradiction everywhere: between the laws of nature and the dictates of conscience, between fact and theory, and in the multiplicity of individual consciousnesses which can only be joined together by force or by false pretences. God is the identification of the ideal with the real; but such as the world is, does it not display to us a kind of insuperable contradiction between the ideal and the real? So the atheist is not atheist by conviction, but merely says that man is condemned to live in an atheist world, devoid of God. Sartre, with some insight, finds the negation of God in the irreducible opposition between value, which has so little strength it is confounded with nothingness, and reality, which is so strong as to be altogether too much. And since evil is basically schism, separation, breaking away, this sort of atheism, as we have already noted, takes up again with a lively aggressiveness the ancient objection of the fact of evil. It is from absolute evil that integral atheism infers the impossibility of God.

So integral atheism is a formidable refutation of philosophies of history of Hegelian or Marxist type that resolve the ancient problem in terms of a "cosmodicy" or "anthropodicy" which is only a cheap form of theodicy. Oppression and war, the blind misery of the alienated masses, the excesses of the privileged classes, violent political and social battles; all forms of evil, in short, find their justification and absolution in the development of humanity, which must follow this dialectical way to attain to its ultimate fulfilment. This is to cheapen concrete individuals thus sacrificed to the system. Atheism thus becomes that moral absolutism which denies in the God of theism and in the God of pantheism the impossible justification of unjustifiable evil.

A better example of this moral absolutism than Sartre, whose thought is spoilt by an affectation of cynicism, a taste for profanity and political impatience, is to be found in the works of Albert Camus. Here we leave the devil's kitchen, and the alembic distils a pure and strong spirit. Camus had no equal in tearing to pieces in beautiful style the systems derived from Hegel which were used to cloak some established tyrannies. Justice, reason, fellowship—these are so many values which demand witness and service, but which prove senseless a world which denies them or, what is worse, is indifferent to them. Camus could not agree that the problem of evil was solved, either by a history irresistibly moving towards perfection, or by the mystery of a God who had already judged, avenged and absolved. Should we not prefer the tragedy of an insoluble problem to a play which, if its ending is written before man has played his part, is really a comedy? The supreme argument is between Christianity and integral atheism. Totalitarian systems and earthly religions only prolong the conflict, which is indeed serious and fraught with danger, between Christianity and paganism. Their clash can take the form of persecution and martyrdom, and it demands courage and spiritual integrity to endure it, but the argument is already settled on earth and in heaven. The last and greatest fight for and against God is fought on higher ground, on that spiritual field where the powers that come from God seem to be turned against God and cause doubt and anguish and suffering in the heart. Leaving the ultimate question unanswered, we can at least conclude here that atheism, whether political or moral absolutism, is a house divided against itself. But whether it is the prime mover of political revolution or the principle of a metaphysical revolt, atheism is not a fleshless system of thought: it is, above all in this century, a historical force. We can therefore ask whether the dialectic of disjunction which seems to be the true essence of atheism allows us to understand its actual fate in the history of our time and to understand the meaning of that history itself.

THE SPIRIT OF MODERN TIMES

THE LAW OF THREE STAGES

The outstanding fact about the world we live in is that atheism has become a political force of such magnitude and power that it is like a rising tide. The moment of change is easily marked: the nineteenth century died in the summer of 1914, when the shots rang out that killed an Austrian archduke and a French Socialist, Jean Jaurès, pacifist orator and humanist. The old political order crumbled, and with it passed also the new Utopias, clearing the way for a new age, which began in October, 1917, when a professional revolutionary, a theorist of political violence who had hammered out and sharpened Marxism to make it into a useful tool for action, seized a decaying empire, collected its strength again, and gave it an imperialist and missionary zeal. After the revolution, in less than fifteen years, Eurasia was for most of its enormous extent conquered for Marxism, and became the colossal crucible in which was produced a Communist civilization and an atheist culture. About a third of mankind, about a thousand million souls, endured the tremendous social pressure of a materialism holding all temporal and spiritual power. The State was identified with an atheist church which strictly regulated the inspiration of men's minds and the direction of their consciences. The party, which officers the people and commands the will of the masses, is a kind of order of chivalry. Its members, who are at the same time administrators, builders and soldiers, are animated by a conviction at once scientific and religious, such that it casts out all doubt and resists all argument from without. For this ruling class, atheism is a first requirement. In that third of the world it is impossible for a believer to have any effective part in public affairs or to make a place for himself among those who govern those affairs. Except, of course, for cases of skilful or heroic pretence. In the Communist system no one can reach the dignity of active citizen without professing atheism implicitly or explicitly. Religion is persecuted or used according to the political needs of the time or the advantage of the moment. The essential point is that this worship which is generally allowed and this God who is forbidden to come out of church or synagogue or mosque are treated as folk-survivals, vestiges of the past which just manage to survive into the present, like a derelict ship stranded on the beach which can never again set out on the deep. And this contrived tolerance, sometimes good-natured, more often contemptuous, is the most Machiavellian intolerance.

This powerful position occupied by atheism raises some anxious questions. A force is powerful less because of what it has done than because of what it can still do. Communism is an all-embracing creed which, like Islam in earlier centuries, joins in a single will to expand spiritual and temporal ambition. Its leaders believe in the infallibility of the Book received from Marx and Lenin; and for its prophecies to be accomplished it is necessary that all men shall one day be Communists. A third of humanity, another thousand million men, are tempted to think of their proletarian condition and of their hope for liberation in terms of Marxist ideology. In the liberal countries of the West, if Marxism has miscarried, even if it is sufficiently refuted by economic growth and human progress brought about without revolution, yet the freedom to question and criticize a society called capitalist and bourgeois is at once both its unique strength and its greatest weakness. It is only lukewarm in its own assertiveness and is hesitant in gambling on the future. Communism, in so far as it is so firmly and aggressively established in the world, seems to be a proof of at least the practical uselessness of religion and of at least the temporal efficiency of atheism. And if Marxism goes on expanding, will not history become a tremendous proof of the non-existence of God?

Communism was not born by spontaneous generation. It opposed Christian civilization from within, issuing from it in a dialectical way by negation and rejection. Everything points to the belief that this civilization, in order for such a radical challenge to have an excuse and a semblance of justification, must already have been stricken by some unseen malady, slow to evolve but latently developing and capable of warning an experienced or inspired observer of the sharp attack of atheism which was coming. For the God the atheism of Nietzsche or Marx dismisses with or without ceremony is the Christian God: the God who became man through love of man and who founded a visible Church, and who is thus caught up in the movement of human history. Gathered together in the Church, Christians are God's chosen people, the new Israel. It is chiefly through their witness and by their action that the knowledge of God and salvation in Christ are to be set before mankind. But the work Christians do in the world is exposed to the perils of the world; it is opposed by the Enemy, whose mark is seen in the idols of those outside the Church, but who acts also in a more secret and more certain way within the fold through the faint-hearted and the faithless, heretics and schismatics. The Christian world, as we are told often enough by philosophers and theologians, is neither God nor the Church: but it can imperil God and the Church. The witnesses called by God can, by becoming hard of heart or through the decay of their faith, become witnesses for the prosecution against God. Our theology of history, which deliberately assumes a prophetic office, since it does not scruple to criticize God's chosen people in the name of a strict and pure service of God, tends to explain the progress of militant atheism in the contemporary world by the deficiencies and deviations of a civilization at first truly and then more and more doubtfully Christian. And as pathology has its own order, and the stages of a disease follow one another with a recognizable connection between them, there is proposed a sort of law of three stages, the substance of which is to be found in most Catholic philosophies of history.

The Middle Ages, the age of Christendom, when even secular life was closely related to God and to religion, constitutes the first or theocratic stage. Modern times are the second or anthropocentric stage: in it man tends to reclaim his autonomy and to make himself the centre and the pinnacle of things, or at least of those activities proper to him. This is shown in the Renaissance, in the Reformation, and in the French Revolution—all great outbursts characteristic of this second stage. If ordinary words were used in their normal sense this modern age would be the real "Middle Ages", the intermediate age in which a fine beginning fails, while the plots are woven unseen which will fill the stage in the last act. This contemporary era, which our civilization has just entered upon, should also be characterized by both irritation with, and the destruction of, the modern age. Anthropocentrism, at first respecting God in order to be able to manage man's affairs, shows its true colours and turns against both God and man. So this is a time of anti-theism and atheism, and also a time of apocalyptic threat and of the tragic probing into man's nature by art and philosophy and political theory. But the proximity of evil gives new opportunties for good. Man may be destroyed or buried alive in some totalitarian anthill; but he might also discover or remake a humanist and theocentric civilization, so that on the horizon of our times there also appears the possibility of a "new Middle Ages" or a "new Christendom", as Berdyaev and Maritain have said. The law of three stages redeems the pessimism of its downward curve by the great hope of its ending: the third stage has not yet said its last word, it is still preparing.

Besides the fact that its last stage is vague and indeterminate, the law of three stages is open to several interpretations, not all equally valid. According to the simplest interpretation, the first stage represents the pattern of successful balance and wisdom, thanks to the sovereignty of God maintained over art and thought and all forms of public and private life. After the peak of the thirteenth century, after the times of St Louis and St Thomas Aquinas, the downward slide begins, the great drift into modernism. At first insensibly, and equivocally, then more and more clearly, Western civilization has been separated from God and led, through various forms of in-differentism and anti-clericalism, to the inevitable extremity of atheism.

From the fourteenth to the twentieth century, even if honour has been preserved by the saints, and the ancient Church—accused of wearisome harping on the same string because she repeats her ancient prayers—has been the unheeded Cassandra prophesying evils to come, yet the most obvious leaders of thought and action, the great men in the eyes of the world, must, if account be taken, be admitted to be those who challenged and destroyed the wisdom of Christianity, who sold off the old stock of theocentric humanism. They have been the nominalists of the fourteenth century, enemies of reason, who introduced fideism into theology and put out the eyes of faith, reducing it to a blind certitude; or those who under the colours of reform and return to Gospel Christianity stirred up heresies which disturbed the spiritual home of all from within and split Christendom. They have been those Renaissance humanists who carefully cultivated the air of loving and learned research into antiquity, while they invented out of nothing a pagan religion of nature and of the will to power; scientists and philosophers of the seventeenth and eighteenth centuries who wanted to reserve to man, whose mind was now well armed with mathematics, whose hand was well aided by machines, the mastery and the possession of a silent world in which no one recognized or wanted to recognize any trace of God. They have been those also, the philosophers of the age of enlightenment, whose deism was only a weapon to be used against the incarnate God and against Churches too long established; the revolutionaries of 1789, theorizing about the rights of man, yet so deliberately forgetful of the duties of man towards God or the rights of God over man. And they have been the liberal economists, theoreticians of a system of self-interest and of profit-making, who under the pretext of not interfering with the free play of impartial laws, gave industrial society a lesson in materialism it will not forget. All these have found heirs and disciples in every generation; and all have helped to build the modern world. Even if some of them were nominal or even sincere Christians, they were in their ignorance of what they were doing the precursors of the great triumphs of atheism in our own century. All revolutions since the sixteenth century are related to one another; whatever their apparent cause or purpose, political or social, they all derive from the same anthropocentrism, the same metaphysical rebellion of man usurping the place of God. At the end justice and logic supervene: forgetfulness of God provokes the denial of God. The saying of the Marxists is very near the truth, that the liberal, secular world, in stirring up atheist Communism, produced its own gravediggers. So the judgement of God is shown in history.

If such an interpretation were correct, there would be no other hope for civilization than a total and complete restoration of the Middle Ages. Only so could man redeem this enormous apostasy to which the modern age is reduced, both in temporal and spiritual things. If in fact the second stage of man's history had been purely and simply a denial, the only means of denying the denial would be to erase the erasure and go back to the initial assertion. Since this is clearly a Utopian idea, the only other possible outcome of the law of three stages to be foreseen is a catastrophic eschatology. But such a philosophy of history as we have briefly outlined, even if it attracts some Christians who react against their own critical times, is indefensible and is now in fact less and less defended. To look upon medieval Christendom as a sort of "thesis" over-whelming the poor and mistaken "hypotheses" of our times is a poetic idealization which might well come back to a mythical resentment against the present. The Middle Ages certainly saw a great attempt to integrate all human life under the laws and universal authority of the Church, but it was by no means a wisdom become historical fact which put an end to history. Jacques Maritain has shown clearly that in those cen-turies of religion insufficient attention was paid to the values of the created world, to the resources proper to God's creatures, to all the depth there was in human subjectivity. It is therefore impossible, unless time is to flow backwards, to make a pattern out of the Middle Ages for a "new Christendom"; there would at least be needed, and this is the theme of Maritain's *True Humanism*, a great change in the meaning of Christendom and in the meaning of humanism, to take into account all that the last four centuries have added to civilization in the field of scientific knowledge.

The anthropocentrism of the second stage is thus not to be summarily rejected as the simple and fundamental contrary of that theocentrism which is a matter of course for the Christian. It is equivocal and susceptible of opposing interpretations. Maritain showed this with a power of reasoning and a felicity of expression which made *True Humanism*[1] a great book, now more than ever. To imagine that the course of history runs counter to the will of God with increasing boldness is to confuse Christianity with Manicheism. From the sixteenth century on-wards there appeared in the history of the West a new interest in man and in man's capabilities, which could and ought to have been assumed into a Christian-inspired synthesis. Accord-ing to Maritain, the principles and the spirit of that synthesis are in the work of St Thomas Aquinas: certainly he repre-sents the highest point of medieval thought, but his real

[1] Published in Spanish in 1934, n French in 1936, and in an English translation by M. R. Adamson (Geoffrey Bles, The Century Press), in 1938.

amplitude is misunderstood if his spirit is confused with the spirit of a particular period.

Maritain used another singularly enlightening term when he called the second stage a "reflective age",[2] one of man's turning back to himself. Let it be said again, this need not necessarily be impious, for the Christian God, God incarnate, God who assumed our nature and lived our life, could not be jealous of man. Yet the risk was enormous. If modern man was not wrong to claim back his rights as an autonomous subject and a. creative personality, in order to make for himself a science and a political theory and a whole culture free from direct relations with religion, yet he was wrong to think of taking this leap ahead of the older culture according to a narrow anthropocentrism, and to imagine that the greater place given to man, the better part won by man, would necessarily produce a compensatory lessening of the place and part of God. So it is that in trying to gain too much in his own self-idolatry man loses all. Narrow anthropocentrism is not humanism, but turns back against man. This explains the crisis of our times. Man who boasts of having created science and of being the subject of his own knowing becomes the object of that science and that knowing. Darwin and Freud soon humbled such pride, by discovering all that is sub-human in man. Marx pitilessly stripped off the material determinants of noble convictions and lofty sentiments. Individualist democracy, which arose out of the Declaration of the Rights of Man and thought in its simple pride that it settled the future direction of history, saw advancing against it the democracy of the masses, taught by Marx, which spurned personal rights as being as worthless as individual privileges. Lastly, the anti-clericalism and secularism of the bourgeois world was at the same time opposed by and

[2] The Reformation, although it ran counter to the Renaissance in having so deeply religious a sense of the absolute sovereignty of God, yet belongs, according to Maritain, to this modern, reflective age, in so far as it asks the creature, man, to seek in his direct meeting with the Lord a pleasure properly his own in his tragically dependent and fallen existence. Cf. *True Humanism*, pp. 8 ff.

fulfilled in the atheist clericalism and totalitarianism of the world of Communism. So, to join together the thought of two masters of the philosophy of history, atheism becomes one of the most characteristic symptoms of what Romano Guardini called "the end of the modern world", a sign that a third stage has begun, that our civilization has entered on a new age.

The law of three stages is true in so far as it has established that the modern world arose out of a breakdown of medieval Christendom which was both fortunate and unfortunate. It is tempting to think, but by no means demonstrated, that the crisis of our times is analogous to the crisis of the Middle Ages, and that a third civilization is emerging out of this modern era by the play of a dialectical negation. Since the law of three stages can be used with different meanings, it cannot solve by itself the problem of the origins of contemporary atheism, but at least it asks the question in the right way: do the idea of the world and the conception of man's existence characteristic of modern times really bear in themselves any germinal notions of atheism, notions at first watered down and disguised and unaware of themselves, but today openly declared and virulent? In a law of three stages it is always the second which is the link and enables us to understand the passage from one stage to another. By almost unanimous consent, our age is dominated or even constituted by a strong leaning towards anthropocentrism: this is evident especially in two fields, that of science and technology and that of political theory. In both fields the claim made to autonomy is made as much for the object as for the subject: that natural world investigated by the scientist and harnessed by the technologist, the state which makes and manages the prince—and according to democratic theory the whole people is the prince—are now seen to be purely secular and temporal and to be quite free from any relationship to religion or the spiritual realm, so that man, scientist and technologist, prince and citizen, wants to assure for himself the lawful possession of, and unrestrained dominion over, that secular nature and temporal state. Now is this anthropocentrism bound to end in atheism? The question is the more important since, as has now been shown, contemporary atheism also professes to be an "integral humanism", to use Maritain's phrase; it asserts that the reign of man excludes the kingdom of God. So some thinking first about science and then about political theory has now become necessary.

IS NATURE NATURAL?

That science is atheist is an official dogma throughout the length and breadth of the Communist world. Since nature is explained by natural causes, God is merely the x of our ignorance and is sufficiently disproved by the advance of human knowledge. Worship and prayer are attitudes of powerlessness: their empty futility is demonstrated by the successes of man's technology. The Soviet *sputnik*, having escaped from that form of alienation which earthly heaviness doubtless is, spins through the immensities of space without coming across angels or God, and the Communist press is not slow in seeing this as proof that the heavens are empty and shall now declare only the glory of man, of Communist man, for to use the forms of atheist apologetics, this triumphant flight was made possible by "a fuel called Socialism". An anti-religious museum in the Soviet Union displays as an argument against the faith the movement of a Foucault pendulum, an experimental and as it were visible proof of the rotation of the earth. Hence it is obvious that since Galileo was right in his dispute with that arch-enemy of science the Church it will be enough for science to make progress to kill God!

The solid dogmatism of such propaganda is a good target for sarcasm, but though it may be contemptibly vulgarized, the scientific argument behind it is not without its point and its effect. We must not lightly take it for a piece of stupidity offered quite properly to the stupid. The attempt to equate natural science with the whole of human wisdom does not fail to stir very deep desires in man. If the case of Galileo has become the spearhead of the scientific attack on apologetics, this is because of a fairly accurate feeling for those difficulties and tensions where vulnerability is to be expected. The story would be pointless if it only concerned the conflict, always and everywhere possible, between established authority and freedom of research: and we all know how the Communist world, where freedom waits on authority, has had many of its own Galileos. The true point of the actual case of Galileo is that it occurred just when medieval Christendom was giving place to the modern world, a period of transition the capital importance of which in the history of civilization the law of three stages has been right in stressing. With Galileo and mathematical physics there was destroyed an idea of the world which a too long association had identified with the Christian faith. The fear grew, and was ever exploited because it is ever exploitable, that the newly revealed natural world would be one without God, as the cosmologies which made medieval man feel safe wavered and disappeared.

The challenge to the geocentric idea was really a very startling shock. At one blow man literally lost his ancient place and became a wanderer in the universe. The motion that carries him along, although it is completely measurable and predictable, is like all motions described mathematically by physics in being perpetual and endless and therefore apparently meaningless. The old closed universe burst open and nature lost its consecrated value, losing itself in a uniform, undifferentiated infinity wherein the same things were endlessly repeated. ("Why here rather than there?" Pascal asked: no one can give clear and careful consideration to the science of his time without also considering Pascal's work.) Nature was no longer natural but indeterminate; man no longer found in nature the familiar landmarks, but wandered lost. Indeed, long before Sartre one could well wonder—as Pascal did early in his work— whether man was not really *de trop* in this world.

A similar trouble arose two centuries later, when evolution began to seem more and more likely to be the truth about life's story. The shadow of a possible repetition of the Galileo affair lay over all that quarrel about evolution, a quarrel which set not only believers against unbelievers but believers themselves against one another. And if the threatened clash remained only a threat, the credit goes to the wisdom of the Church and the prudence of the real scientists involved, and also to real and substantial progress in Christian philosophy. The theory of evolution shifted a fixed point which until then had seemed a firm image of eternal truth: time was drawn out behind us, age being accumulated upon age in an unheard-of manner, just as space had expanded to infinity around the contemporaries of Galileo and Pascal. Life was no longer the great Mother, holy and always the same: it disappeared, dissolved into elements less and less specialized as time moved back to a far distant past. Living things were no longer arranged in order in a completely harmonious whole, but were simply snatched up in a sort of vortex out of which man was produced, a shell cast up on the shore. So organic nature also seemed to be indeterminate and no longer natural, just as inorganic nature had. The theory of evolution and the investigation of the biological origins of man have in the last hundred years produced the same loss of man's equilibrium as did formerly the end of heliocentrism, the question of the plurality of worlds, and the empty silences of interstellar space. In each case the trouble is explicable in the same way: the accustomed signature of God, or what was taken to be the divine signature, was no longer to be seen in a world which could be called desecrated,[3] and desecrated by science. So we must grant to scientific atheism, of which Marxism is today the only historically important expression, that the progress of science has put traditional belief in God to the test.

But at the same time it challenges man's belief in himself:

[3] "Desecrated", and the verb "to desecrate", used in this translation for the French *désacralisé, désacraliser*, are to be understood throughout in the older and more proper sense of "to take away its sacred character from; to treat as not sacred" (*Concise Oxford Dictionary*)—*Trans.*

nature is insecure, God is insecure, but so is man. Adrift on a
flood the source or direction of which he cannot know scientifically, involved in a network of ordered and completely determinate causes and effects, man may wonder whether science does
not prove Lucretius and Epicurus right after all, and whether
the world—this desecrated world—is not really a vast accident,
and man only the latest accidental effect of a more ancient
accident. So what we have so far said about modern anthropocentrism, basing ourselves on Maritain and others, must be
made to stretch, must be subtly amended in this present context.
Indeed, science sternly rejects any anthropocentrism as it were
written materially into things. So much so that man today
must anxiously wonder what is his place in a natural world
which no longer consecrates him naturally as its lord and king.
Hence there arises a new anthropocentrism of which man and
man alone is the inventor and sole beneficiary. If the universe
itself is blind, surely must man be proud, even inordinately
proud, of being the only light in the universe, of being the
one without whom the recession of the galaxies and the ascent
of life would have remained buried in their darkness? And if
the earth is indifferent to being inhabited or uninhabited,
and indifferent to the social condition of its inhabitants, surely
man, who knows he can grasp the earth and organize it to his
own profit, surely he will think of himself as its only inhabitant,
as the lawful possessor of this ownerless source of profit,
which, what is more, his labour can bring to bear fruit? This
would seem to be the origin of the rationalism and the Promethean spirit typical of our times. In a world which science has
secularized, where we can no longer see any handy signposts
pointing towards God, the void is so vast that man, the whole of
man, and more, is needed to fill it. Nature no longer has a
natural centre, so man must be its artificial centre. The artificiality is conscious, and so it is known to be a sort of trick, so
that there is something forced about modern anthropocentrism.
Nature makes man insecure, but he tries to throw off that
insecurity by arbitrarily setting himself up as God. Hence,

paradoxically, a certain arbitrariness and violence which appear in modern rationalism. It is not surprising that *sputniks*, as products of an arbitrary power, preach atheist rationalism throughout space in a universe desecrated, dehumanized, void of divinity.

Shaken by this secularization by which science discovers the truths of nature, belief in God and the sense of the holy come out of the test able to regard science more closely, not only purified but also strengthened. Modern science cannot prove God's existence, and to argue against the idea that there is such a scientific proof is to batter at a door already open. Natural science does indeed, by supposing at each step that there is no such absolute and holy reality as Nature, cast out from our minds and our systems of ideas that great Idol which falsifies and perverts the idea of God, and which we can see being refashioned at the very heart of dialectical materialism. There is in fact a strong temptation to treat nature as a great Being encompassing all beings including man, or as a holy thing worthy of piety and reverence, as a necessary intermediary between God and man, greater than man but hardly less than God; it may even be identified with God himself. Ancient man believed in the divinity of Nature. Epicurus and Lucretius were received very badly by their contemporaries partly, it is true, because they made pleasure the good, but mainly because they dared, which was much more distasteful to the orthodox, not to believe in the eternity of the world or its divine soul. Plotinus, so good an example both of the greatness and of the limits of Greek culture, was on this account actively hostile to the Christians of his time,[4] who carried their barbarity of spirit and their lack of respect for the beauty of this world so far as to grant to the meanest slave that soul they denied to the visible divinity of the world. The very first verse of the Bible overthrows the greatest idol of the Gentiles, since if the world is the work of God as Creator it cannot be God himself.

4 More strictly, Plotinus, in the texts we refer to, was arguing against the Gnostics, but their ideas were obviously derived from Christianity.

But pagan ideas die hard, and medieval cosmology was often contaminated by unfortunate survivals from antiquity.

It might be relevant to mention that inquiry into the world and the idea of nature was always a source of argument throughout the history of Christian thought. Platonists and Aristotelians, Augustinians and Thomists, gave different accounts of the world and different meanings to nature. From the point of view of a *philosophia perennis* which means to preserve everything, even such scholastic arguments, it is the fact of this argument which has doctrinal implications. Faith in God the Creator constitutes a challenge to the idea of nature, and so opens the way to scientific advance. And it is significant that the founders of modern science belonged to the Platonist and Augustinian tradition, in which that challenge took the boldest critical form; the philosophy natural to science is not naturism. But this is a digression. It is still true that even if science cannot prove by its own resources and methods that the world was created by God, it nevertheless puts out of court all forms of paganism, whether openly avowed or shame-facedly covert. Science leaves no room for poetic truth, pays honour to no spirit hidden in material things, knows neither soul of the world nor spirit of life; but it indirectly opens up a glimpse of God's transcendence and of his creation, not indeed as demonstrated certainties, but as real possibilities now that all restrictions have been removed. Science has certainly killed God—but it is the pagan God of Nature. The great god Pan is twice dead: first and foremost at the hands of Genesis and the Gospels, but also, and it is an important addition, at the hands of modern science.

The paradoxical situation produced by modern science hopelessly contradicts all pagan naturism, but also and as hopelessly atheism of the type of dialectical materialism. It must be insisted that man cannot wholly be comprehended by a nature now "demythologized" and no longer an all-embracing totality. However rooted he may be in the world, man always emerges from it, at least because of the consciousness he has of his own roots. So far as concerns man, evolutionary biology falls in with physics, which is mechanist today as it was yesterday. As the theory of evolution is ever more strongly established as an important biological truth, and man thinks of himself as the culmination of the long, slow ascent of life, the undeniable fact of his being rooted in evolution, by becoming an object of knowledge and of spiritual concern, demonstrates the emergence of reflection, of self-conscious intelligence. For man, by postulating the theory of evolution as true and then asking whether life has meaning or not, gives a philosophical twist to science and separates himself in mind from that life to which he is biologically and materially bound. Plunged into life, man makes an approach to it but in the very act withdraws from it. The late Fr Teilhard de Chardin unfailingly upheld this position. He never considered life, biologically, as a being existing in itself, a sort of intermediate divinity confirming the creation and the consecration of man, but always saw the *raison d'être* of life in mind, for life without mind would be meaningless and absurd.[5] Evolution, indeed, may explain the whole story of life, but not the mental act of a Bergson or a Teilhard de Chardin, reflectively philosophizing with inspired felicity on evolution. It is thus clearly impossible to integrate man fully into nature. But the alternative is wrong which would force us to choose between integration and complete independence. The phenomenon of man is unalterably rooted in nature, and there will never be an end to the list of material, biological and sociological factors which condition him and which allow a scientific account of him to be given. But in so far as he practises science, as he makes scientific judgements and engages in effective enquiry, man is no longer only a phenomenon, he knows that he is a free subject. The more science advances and the more man's roots in nature are seen to be firmly and solidly

[5] This idea of mind as the *raison d'être* of life is very typical of the powerfully apologetic philosophy of Fr Teilhard. But it should be said that he tended to make it more an objective and scientific truth than a truly reflective one.

fixed, the clearer is man's emergence, and this duality[6] is the very state of man. Not that there are two men in man. The roots and the top make up the one being. This duality does not itself imply any particular philosophy, and it is not necessary to decide now whether it is a paradox, an absurdity or a mystery. It is sufficient now to see that man, after the test of science, is no more natural than is nature itself.[7] Now Marxist atheism throws all its weight into forcing nature and man to admit that they are fully and wholly natural. Obviously this attitude is not Christian, but it is equally clear that it ill accords either with the spirit of the modern world or with that of science.

So the modern world professes an uncertain anthropocentrism. It is known, with the certainty of scientific knowledge, that man is a latecomer and an upstart in nature, the child of the working of nature; and there is a flagrant contrast, if

[6] This duality was made part of seventeenth-century philosophy by Descartes and Pascal, who thus ingeniously reconciled Christian and scientific thinking. Not all the good effects of their successful effort have been realized, and too many Catholic writers have been unfair to it and ungrateful for it, because they have not always exactly comprehended the content and intentions of that philosophy, which was both Christian and modern. It is quite obvious, for example, despite deep-rooted scholastic prejudice, that duality does not mean dualism, except and only except in method. Descartes's man is at once one and double, which is a fair description of man as man and Christian. But I should here admit that my opinion is opposed by the authority of philosophers of such different inclinations as Jacques Maritain and Gabriel Marcel.

[7] The felicitous expression "nature is unnatural" is used and explained in depth by Romano Guardini in *The End of the Modern World* (translated by J. Theman and H. Burke, Sheed and Ward, 1957). Guardini thinks that this "denaturalization" of nature should be characteristic of the third stage of our civilization, implying a break with the picture of the universe the modern world has built up. But such rash apologias for the divinity of nature as are met in many streams of Renaissance and Romantic thought are survivals from antiquity. It seems to me, as opposed to Guardini, that the expression "nature is unnatural", which is so typical of Descartes or Pascal, takes on its true meaning and importance not at the end but at the beginning of the modern era. It could also be said that for modern times nature is just nature and nothing more; such terms are less pregnant and conceal the magnitude of the revolution or the discovery.

not a contradiction, between the little or nothing he is by nature and the whole he claims to become by his action. Now it is the task of dialectical materialism to cast off and bury and to deny the existence of this particular worry. Marxist neo-positivism demands that science expand into a complete system of knowledge, capable of reconciling man with himself and with nature. Marxists call this universally encompassing reality matter: since it encompasses all it must therefore encompass man also. It is really no other than the ancients' Nature, that very Nature which science has once for all done away with. We are told that this matter is essentially dialectical, that its process of becoming is auto-dynamic and submitted to the laws of contradiction and of progress by leaps forward, by sudden jumps. Besides the fact that such laws have nothing scientific in their content, they belong in spirit to a sort of poetic mythology, in which we can discern the pagans' primacy of Nature over man.

Auto-dynamism is a property of things, inhuman or super-human, as you will; it is material, yet orientated towards improvement. Contradiction and progress by forward leaps are the dramatic substance of all that is, they are the keys opening the way to the understanding and prediction of all changes in all fields, physical as well as historical, and these preliminary dogmas impose their authority on judgements and action alike. If, for example, reform is detestable and true politics are revolutionary, this is because of the law of progress by forward leaps, which is a law of nature as a whole and so also, as a corollary or by application, of human society. Reasoning correctly according to dialectical materialism always means starting from a whole of which the human is only one category. Marxist atheism is obsessed by a longing for the divine, even if it expresses a deliberate desire to replace God by matter. For matter is understood by Marxism in a sense more metaphysical and more mythical than truly scientific: it is the first, immanent cause of all things, within which unfolds a whole chain of effects bound together by necessity which always remain contained and sustained by their cause.

Everything new in the world is thus a property of this unique substance, an unfolding of its dynamic potentialities, even the thought of Marx and the political genius of Lenin, since life and mind are only dialectical developments of matter, which literally fulfils the role of God. The forward-looking re-assurance of the Marxist catechism must be looked at from the other end, and dialectical materialism seen as a retrograde step, even compared with the materialism of the eighteenth century or the mechanism of Democritus, which had at least the merit of making matter an objective and scientific idea. The Marxists' matter changes their atheism into pantheism: it is an absolute divinity not so far removed, if we may compare something so vague with such an exact concept, from what Spinoza called substance, self-caused, pure and active nature. In this way dialectic makes a show of solving the problem of the divine attributes. Adhering to the world and its laws by "praxis", which is thought as well as action, man is freed from all metaphysical torment, being dogmatically assured that he is moving with the universe, that is, is in agreement with God. God or nature. A back-flash from ancient pantheism.

The Promethean emergence of man described by Marx, in which is to be found the spirit of the modern world, is incompatible with a system of natural or physical materialism, which directly puts Prometheus out of court. In the history of ideas dialectical materialism represents a retrogressive move-ment towards the pagan and mythical forms of antiquity. It is not just anti-Christian, but pre-Christian; not just anti-scientific, but pre-scientific—a shocking disgrace for a "pro-gressive" creed! For it claims to unite and to subordinate man to that kind of nature, and science to that sort of wisdom, which Christianity and science have done away with, by two liberating processes different in their origins and in their aims but analogous in their results. Marxism, which fails to be modern in its Promethean ideas, is anti-modern in its dialectical materialism. Hegel's nostalgia for ancient Greece lies heavily on the shoulders of his most prominent disciples.

In brief, Marxist atheism solved the problem of God without ever really posing it—leaving aside some intuitions of Marx's youth—and solved it by using a poetic mythology of nature dead for two thousand years. Only the man (and he is in fact modern in his formation and in his thinking) who seeks but does not find in nature an answer to his highest questioning, only he really faces the problem of God honestly and squarely, and then he has to decide between solitude and the supreme confrontation. Marxism stops short of this choice, stops this side of that great argument, and by its political strength makes up—or rather, fails to make up—for its intellectual and spiritual poverty. It is as if Communist atheism, in face of the fair questioning and real powers of modern man, is nothing but an enormous attempt to avoid the issues by putting the clock back.

THE POLITICAL MISUSE OF RELIGIOUS IDEAS

As we have so easily shown, atheism in its Marxist form is by no means an inevitable result of that desecration of nature effected by modern science. But could it be regarded as the necessary and final consequence of that increasing desecration of society effected by modern political theory, and by the growing secularization of public life? There appear to be good reasons for so regarding it, reasons we must now examine.

In medieval times a Christian civilization asserted itself in history. Christian princes and Christian principles ruled men and the actions of men, with the pope and the emperor, the "two halves of God", at the top of the structure of society. Power was only legitimate so far as it was recognized by the Church and consecrated by a God whose sovereignty was an article of both religious and political faith. Modern times, on the contrary, have separated spiritual and temporal, Church and State, often so effectively that neither knows anything of the other. Unbelief, sceptical or dogmatic, has gone so far that for very many people reference to religion neither reinforces civic duty nor justifies patriotism: both must now find their basis on earth and not in heaven. The unity of the faith has given ground more and more to the practical plurality of religious sects. So nations must now fashion each for itself a soul, with common values no longer those of religion, which is commonly accused of dividing more than it unites. While God seems more and more remote, the State becomes wholly secular, and refuses to consider itself as the secular arm of any church. Politics has become a purely profane affair. So this modern age has replaced the medieval synthesis by a systematic dualism. But is not to reduce the rôle of God in man's life to prepare the way for the denial of God altogether?

The French Revolution seems to have been the practical source of this secularization of public life. It followed Rousseau in proclaiming the sovereignty of the people. This became the foundation of a new system of law and seemed to deny the sovereignty of God, for it made the general will the supreme arbiter of good and evil and the basis, which can properly be called godless, a-theist, of man's authority over his fellows. By proclaiming freedom of worship, freedom of the press and freedom of speech, and by submitting spiritual affairs to a sort of competitive society, a kind of bargaining existence, revolutionary ideology surely gave equal chances, and hence equal worth, to truth, which is in a way unique and total, and to countless forms of error. Public authority no longer prohibited debates about God's existence. Was not religious belief degraded, reduced to the level of opinion along with other beliefs? Was not this to declare that since God's existence was in fact debated, it was therefore publicly recognized as debatable? The Rights of Man, asserted as so many absolute necessities, supposed that the creature man had in him and in himself alone the source and principle of his moral dignity. This was an anthropocentrism which did scant justice to creation and to grace, that is, to God himself. Certainly Rousseau and the revolutionaries of 'eighty-nine and 'ninety-three called the Supreme Being to witness and professed deism; and it is ironic that Robespierre and the Jacobins who persecuted Christians believed more sincerely in God and immortality than Napoleon, the restorer of religion. But their God was never able to found more than a civic religion: he was himself wholly secular. The logic of the new society meant that the God of Christian consciousness became something private, relegated to the secrecy of one's own soul, to the concealment of a worship that was itself only the expression of the interior life, a mere adjunct to private life.

Has not history, moreover, passed judgement on God? From liberal democracy to atheist Communism: it seems a logical sequence. Long ago, Plato taught in Book VIII of his *Republic* that democracy, where the majority was sovereign and the free exchange of opinions replaced the rule of wisdom, was bound to end in a totalitarianism of ideas and the tyranny of the worst elements. Communism blatantly claims to be the heir of liberal democracy, the principles of which Marxism has shown to be merely the ideological disguise of class interest. Freedom of thought, freedom of initiative, freedom of exchange, all make up the same bourgeois idea. The sovereignty of the people will only be real, the rights of man will only be truly rights, when a whole united community has destroyed, along with capitalist economy and private property, all opposition between classes and all divisions into parties, to take charge itself in complete autonomy of the whole of its existence as a society. Such is the end, the completion, of liberal anthropocentrism. And the Communist revolutionary, good pupil as he is of his mortal enemy the bourgeois revolutionary, wants to make himself absolute master of his own future. So the secularism of modern times, a form of practical atheism, or atheism ashamed of itself and so hidden, will become in the Communist age dogmatic atheism, a state religion, the unifying force of a society which will have achieved its political freedom by the death of God. This is the certain end of the secularization of public life.

Such a philosophy of history as has just been outlined cannot give a fair and proper picture of that ideal Christendom which is given a semblance of historical substance by being projected back into an idealized, conventional Middle Ages, nor of the true nature of political atheism, of which Communism is the actualized form, nor of that secularization of life which has been going on throughout the history of the west. "Give back to Caesar what is Caesar's, and to God what is God's" (Matthew 22. 21). That command marks the division between two kinds of society: that kind of politico-religion which deified Caesar was judged and rejected. The modern world may indeed be thought of as having been born on the day when Christianity, not as an essential part of its message and work but as a practically immediate consequence of that message, secularized politics as it also secularized nature: neither was to be confused with the kingdom of God. It was a revolution difficult to see at first, for its seeds were scarcely perceptible. Besides, paganism is not only a worldly system of government: it is permanently on the side of the closed against the open, of material heaviness against spirit. But it cannot now suffice on its own. History took a new turn when the first Christians risked their worldly position and their lives by refusing to pay religious honours to Caesar, as they refused to worship the sun or nature. They showed not only physical courage but also spiritual heroism, for the invincible empire and the everlasting universe were held divine with considerable plausibility by the best citizens and the most important philosophers. When they confessed the true God, the first martyrs were also pioneering a new civilization, which put political society in its proper place by denying that it was the sacred source of all justice and by demanding that it obey laws higher than itself. If the modern world is secular, in that it separates temporal and spiritual, profane and sacred, that secularity is undeniably of Christian origin. It was to be continually questioned and threatened by absolutism, by attempts to revive the political system of antiquity; and this dispute between Christianity and political absolutism throws some light on European history.

From the end of the persecutions to the French Revolution constitutes a period which may be called the Constantinian era. For it was the conversion of the first Christian emperor which gave it its character: Christianity, recognized as the State religion, was on the temporal level a sort of binding force for the political community. Heresy and lack of faith were civil failings in the subject, and in the prince suggested the illegitimacy of his rule and ground for his deposition. After the Reformation and the break-up of Christendom, the tradition that religious unity was essential to political unity remained. Toleration of irreligion or another religion would mean the end of the established order. It would be wrong to see in this Constantinian practice a pure and simple survival of the political ideas of pagan antiquity. The Germanic Holy Roman Empire might try to revive the Rome of the Caesars; late-medieval theories of empire such as those of Dante, which tried to make the world of politics completely self-sufficient, might be cousins german of cosmologies inspired by antiquity and tainted with Averroism, which saw nature as a self-sufficient whole; both political and cosmological theories might be too infatuated with their pre-Christian past: the divine right of kings suggests a confusion, a contamination of true Christian doctrine by pagan Caesarism; but political absolutism was never able to be carried to extremes so long as men confessed the Christian God. The Middle Ages were politically pluralist. The Holy Roman Empire, the doubtful holiness of which inclined to appropriate to itself what was proper to religion, was generally opposed by a good half of Christendom and most often by the papacy itself, keenly defending its spiritual independence. Even when Caesar claimed to be the only vicar of God in this world, religion kept its own province outside of and above politics. There were always furious battles within Christendom between various political ideologies, and the problem of the spiritual and the temporal powers was always acutely presented and variously solved, though never in a totalitarian way. In these conflicts of ideas and authority was formed the political consciousness of western man. Neither of the two powers reduced the other to its mercy. Christianity maintained its universalism and its transcendence through the most terrible trials and sometimes through the most dreadful misunderstandings, and God never became the cult-deity of a closed community. The Constantinian era was still politically a great advance on pagan antiquity.

After the French Revolution the political order became pluralist *de jure* as well as in practice. But the end of the Constantinian era should not be confused with the death of God. The old struggle between Christianity and political absolutism, which we have said is of the essence of European history, continued under new forms. The tension showed itself even within the revolutionary ideology. On the one hand the French Revolution set forth and popularized an individualist philosophy which made the individual man the end of society, and on the other, thinking the time had come to integrate man completely into a wholly rationalized society, it brought into being the first modern totalitarian state. This totalitarianism, reviving as it did the political absolutism of pagan times, was quite incompatible with the individualism, which was basically of Christian origin. The same contradiction which led the French Revolution from the Rights of Man to the Reign of Terror and then to dictatorship could already be seen in the political thinking of its spiritual father, Jean-Jacques Rousseau. In *The Social Contract* he was only so very vehement in opposing right to actuality and liberty to actual slavery in order to construct in the end a totalitarian system in which society laid claim to the whole of a man. He had sufficient insight to criticize—and how forcibly!—the Christian distinction between what belonged to Caesar and what to God, which, he declared, had for so long prevented man from achieving complete political unity. The impossible rule of two powers, in fact, divided man and society. The evil came from the fact that Christ "came to set up on earth a spiritual kingdom which, by separating the theological from the political system, made the state no longer one . . .".[8] For Rousseau, as later for Hegel, Christianity, at least in its political consequences, had corrupted the healthy state of ancient civilization. The remedy could be seen from the diagnosis of the disease: the revolution now necessary was that which should re-establish unity between "the theological system" and "the political system", which should gather into one and the same religion piety towards the State and piety towards the gods or towards the divinity; a revolution which should abolish the distinction between spiritual and temporal powers and so end the disturbing digression introduced into history by Christianity, linking up again with the political and religious traditions of paganism, even if it meant paganizing Christianity by transforming it into a national religion. Logically enough, Rousseau went on to justify the Roman Empire's persecution of Christians, whom the author of *The Social Contract*, following Diocletian, treated as truly guilty of treason.

It is easier to see from all this the real tragedy of the French Revolution and the promises of liberty it gave, and the intolerance implicit in its ideology. The proclamation of the Rights of Man was by no means an attack on God. It is easier to see now that the concept of the Rights of Man had become a commonplace of Christian individualism; even if it was expressed in terms of religious neutrality, it meant that man was not merely a natural phenomenon, not just an atom in the mass of society; beyond a certain point he could not be treated simply as a means but had in him something holy and absolute, in short, a soul, which came to him neither from nature nor from society. But the greatest importance lay in the ambition to construct an entirely new society, rational throughout, which should tolerate

[8] Rousseau, *The Social Contract*, IV, 8: translated G. D. H. Cole, Everyman's Library No. 660 (1913).

neither division nor defection, in which man, promoted to the status of citizen, should find his ultimate fulfilment. This ambition gave a totalitarian content to the idea of the sovereignty of the people, and was a return to that political absolutism which the Judaeo-Christian tradition had always opposed as wrong. It is a kind of law of mutual stimulation of contraries: on the one hand the lively awareness of the basic demands of Christianity, and on the other the irritant, a tenacious survival from paganism. Because of these two violently opposed forces in its divided self the French Revolution prophetically contained the great struggle between them; not altogether a new struggle, but powerfully renewed, and still today holding the future of mankind in the balance. In the conflicts which in our century oppose democracy and totalitarianism as two ways of looking at and living human life, a revolution is fighting against a revolution, and a previously hidden contradiction bursts into the full light of history.

Political absolutism only became conscious of itself by developing the totalitarian component of the French Revolution and rejecting the humanist part. This led to the dropping of the principles of 1789 and some fundamental Christian values; it also led to an ordered settlement after a period of doubt and confusion. And as always thought was ahead of history.

The intention of Hegel was so to revolutionize the Christian God that he became politically useful. For the faith of the Gospels, by reducing the world to a testing-place for man, temporary and somewhat unreal, could only end in political bankruptcy. The God of Jesus Christ, the God of the individual soul, could not be the God of a community. What nation, asked the young Hegel, could say the words of the Lord's Prayer without denying its own strength, without losing its honour in humbly submitting to one greater than itself? The God of the new world should be the God of history, who made strength the sign of rightness, not he who mocked Caesar by offering him a counterfeit coin, spiritually devalued. Simply by making the individual moral conscience absolute, revolutionary idealism made its own realization in history impossible. Man ought to find the spirit of his spirit in society, the reason for his reason in the State. Antigone long ago compromised the fine totality of the ancient city-state by opposing to the high gods, those of the light and of the city, the gods of the underworld, those of the family and of private life. But that unsurpassable masterpiece of wisdom, the city-state, was to be the true goal of future history. So Hegel preached a completely political religion, one which was to be realized in Communism, but also in atheism, thanks to a logic more Hegelian than Hegel's own.

For Auguste Comte also it was a political objection which was more decisive even than the scientific argument in finally overcoming not only the Christian God but also the God of all theology and all metaphysics. For if God existed, mankind could never attain to a fully rational human society; care for his personal salvation, that absolute concern which would be demanded as alone worthy of the divine absolute, would prevent each man devoting himself entirely to the common task, which is political. Since he releases man from the ties which bind him to society and which are all his essential reality, God is impossible on political grounds. Political absolutism destroys the divine absolute, or rather, replaces it with that other absolute, Humanity, in which each man lives and moves and has his being. And for Comte revolutionary individualism is the same enemy as Christian individualism under different colours, metaphysical instead of theological. The principles of 1789, which had served so well in destroying the old order, had only a negative value and would be capable of demolishing any social structure whatever, because of the value they attributed to the individual. One should not speak of "the Rights of Man": it is the same individualist heresy, for the idea of "rights" is as much immoral as absurd. There would at last emerge from the destruction of these two forms of individualism a properly ordered society in which the rule of scientific truth would cut out all freedom of thought, a wholly religious society, in which God would be dead and the devotion of each to the task of all could at last be total and complete. Comte was not day-dreaming; he saw quite clearly what sorts of forces threatened democracy and Christian values. But he thought they had right on their side and would govern the future of man. Comte's positivism was wrong in all its detailed forecasts, but the political absolutism he saw as the fulfilment of history has been realized in Communism.

The distinction often drawn between the political revolution of 1789 and the social revolution of 1917 is very superficial. A revolt of serfs or of peasants is not a revolution: there is only political revolution. By refashioning a society, Marxism gives political substance to economics and social theory. The abolition of private property and the destruction of the class structure result in the over-development of political power and the subordination of private to public life. The State is strengthened by the collected power of a people gathered into a single mass, and its might spreads everywhere over the people, so universally and powerfully active that no greater can be seen elsewhere or even conceived of. Industrial expansion and production records speak a will to power political in its aims as in its spirit. Theories of socialist realism make art and literature weapons in the struggle, instruments of propaganda. A social hierarchy is established following the order of increasing political importance; so much so that the State as a legal entity coincides exactly with the actual country and forms its character, its mind and its will. That man is a political animal is taken to be descriptive of his essential nature, and it is in politics that the ineffable, the absolute, the holy, are now to be found. Argument, opinion and revolt might have some meaning in man's prehistory as peaceful or violent means of bringing about the final stage, but once the leap has been taken and society has entered history, opposition seems sacrilegious and calls upon itself a judgement such as might be given by an inquisition in a "religious" society: error is heresy, disaffection is apostasy, and the punishment is a ritual purification accompanied by curses. Absolute political power has absorbed all the powers of organized religion.

Such political absolutism according to the meaning attributed to the word, is either the contrary of atheism, since a secular religion is one which advances by taking over the functions of religion proper, or is a kind of atheism, not only theoretical but practical and actualized, since a secular religion excludes the religion of the true God, who simply by existing makes nature and society relative and subordinate. Totalitarianism, Fascist, Nazi or Communist, represents the extreme limit of the secularization of man's existence, making man a wholly natural phenomenon, a wholly political animal. It is also the ultimate form of secularism, being pluralist and locating the most precious spiritual good beyond temporal existence, so that even in completely dechristianizing society it consecrates it, after a pagan fashion, while at the same time deprecating all there was of expectancy or unrest in paganism, as with Antigone or Socrates. Dostoevsky saw clearly into the future when he wrote that socialism, as a total solution to the political problem, only had meaning in and through atheism: the religion of the Grand Inquisitor who denies Christ and takes away men's freedom in order to ensure their happiness according to the best approved scientific methods is not a bad personation of Communism.

We could say that Marxism fulfils and completes modern anthropocentrism by making humanity a sort of Godless mystical body which justifies every sacrifice, but that it is also the contrary of anthropocentrism in that it reduces the individual man to the status of a means and instrument. When our age desecrated nature and desecrated society it was not necessarily confessing God, but it realized or had some idea that the best and most secret part of the spirit was to be found neither in nature nor in society, and so admitted the vitality of the Christian leaven in civilization; for if the Gospel is right, man's full destiny is not the same as his natural or political end. His final destiny, which brings him fear and trembling but also greatness and dignity, totalitarianism and Marxism, as political systems and State religions, must fanatically reject, for unless they are to fall into inconsistency and incoherence man must necessarily be completely included in and accounted for by society and nature. It is an attempt at alienation which can never be developed to the full or entirely succeed, since for it to do so it would be necessary to overcome modern man, to overcome man as such: but both stand secure.

WHEN MAGIC IS REMOVED, IS LABOUR ALL?

This is an industrial age, in which machines give man greater and greater mastery over the world, in which labour is visibly creative, in which technological and scientific marvels are of daily occurrence. This world in which man sees himself more and more as master of his own destiny is bound to endanger religious values, and its materialism is bound to weigh heavily against the idea of God. What is gained by technology is lost to mystery. Does not all this, part as it is of the very structure of our civilization, constitute an invitation to atheism?

The technological attitude of mind, as we may call it, if it is not just an attitude but is all there is to the mind, cuts off religious feelings at their roots, destroying the mind's unprejudiced openness to the divine, its contemplative attitude and its avowal of mystery. Intelligence is wholly directed towards useful action: a tool is an idea actualized in matter, and an idea only has meaning as a potential tool. Truth is identified with verifiability. Man's expectation can never do more than anticipate a result predictable because already set out on the drawing board. If this rationalist pragmatism becomes the philosophy natural to the most modern of modern men, factory workers and research scientists, is this not proof that faith and worship, which call for a philosophy of acceptance and consent, have become impracticable for man simply because of the development of a technological society? What is even more serious than a deliberate and considered rejection of God, there is often to be found among the industrial proletariat and in scientific circles a sort of spontaneous, unpremeditated indifference to the problem of God.

To the devaluation of contemplation and worship there corresponds in the mind of modern man an inflation of the value of labour, which makes man the ruler of this world. Labour was unaware of its own proper value while it shared its true nature between asceticism, which made it a means of disciplining the flesh and conquering man's instincts, and mysticism, which only raised it at all in a gesture of sacrifice and oblation. Asceticism and mysticism were well fitted to make it blind to its own strength, which lies in producing practical results and in raising man higher while subordinating nature to man. Then labour expands in a blaze of Promethean glory. Creative fire has been stolen from the gods to inspire a science which is technological, a technology which is scientific, so that mankind is no longer animal, fearful, instinctive and natural, but becomes really and truly humanity. More and more, labour becomes aware of itself; it is no longer only a surer way than instinct of getting pleasure or satisfaction or peaceful sleep, for that does not really raise man above his natural origins; it becomes more and more, as Romano Guardini, for example, has shown, a will to power and domination. The Prometheus myth, which poured a spirit of unrestrained impiety into human labour, is a parable of modern times, clearly explained and commented on by our industrial civilization. We remember that the young Marx thought of labour, which for him was of the very essence of man, as a proof that God did not exist. So technology, by which man discovers his own self-creative power, finds its inevitable philosophy in atheism. Is the thought of Marx exactly in accord with the spirit of modern times on this point?

This is where our previous analyses come together, as though now the secret of modern times is really out. If modern civilization has an irresistible power of secularization, it is because it is a civilization based on labour. Science desecrates nature because it breaks up and remakes its objects in the way in which *homo faber* or an engineer makes tools and machines, reducing matter to equations and so to servitude. Modern politics desecrates society in so far as it makes society the work, and sometimes the titanic construction, of human labour. How can what human ingenuity can make, break and remake point to anything holy and other? The fact and the success of labour must be the most efficient agent in the secularization of the modern world, and the question again arises: does secularization necessarily lead to atheism? The answer has already been given and validated for science and politics: the secularization produced by labour and a technological society is a purifying trial for religion. The fine and noble truths about himself won by man, thanks to the reflection on itself of his Promethean genius, allow the problem of God to be posed in a more urgent and compelling way, freed from all mythology and idolatry. What is truly holy is not obscured or lost because of the transition to the secular implied by the autonomy of human action.

It would be dishonest apologetics to claim Prometheus as a disciple of the true God. But that militant irreligion which makes him side with atheism in revolt risks confusing God with Zeus, jealous of mankind. The atheism of the natural sciences or politics, which makes Prometheus the type of the new man, mistakes his true nature and, like Hermes in the legend, only helps to bind him. The truth is that Prometheus is a question, that and no more: what he rejects is really rejected, but what he promises or asserts is ever vague and uncertain.

Prometheus is the contradiction of paganism within paganism, the myth which signifies the approaching twilight of mythology. Because he labours, man is superior to the gods of nature and to nature itself: how could man worship what is inferior to himself? Science and technology make the same break with that primitive enchantment which filled the world with magic and made man's thinking dark and uncertain as a dream. Prometheus is man awake. Rational prediction of eclipses chases a pagan terror from the sky, and navigation and meteorology end the days of Neptune and the Keeper of the Winds. Prometheus has shown well enough that nature is never equal to man. Civilizations and cultures are equally desecrated by labour, once it knows itself Promethean. They are secular from the moment they are shown on all the evidence to be the work of man. There is a magic about the closed community, the State, a religion almost, which holds men longer than the magic of the natural world; but even that obsession cannot resist the clarity of the Promethean consciousness. The modern citizen knows that the State is the work of citizens, and not the other way round; or rather, that it is always man who acts through society on man. All imaginary terrors withdraw, and for Pascal, who as a Christian knew nothing of the sacredness of nature or political powers, "the mark of the divinity is no more printed on the faces" of princes than it is in the courses of the stars, numbered, measured and weighed by men.[9] History also is entirely secular, made by man: it cannot become a divinity moving inscrutably towards its own ends—like the Nature of the ancients—using man to realize its designs. This would be to make the effect greater than its cause. Henceforth, it is impossible to make a religion of magic and seek refuge in Nature or salvation in society. Prometheus, to use our earlier terminology, is man's emergence, man proving by his own acts that he cannot be wholly the product of Nature or the result of history. But Prometheus' torment is born with him. In the world he has made Prometheus finds neither standard nor purpose. The things he knows and masters by means of machines and equations are only instruments and functions, and man must look elsewhere, if anywhere, for meaning and for peace. Prometheus' power can at any instant call itself and its own effects in question; it is established at the very limits of contingency and insecurity. It is only too well known that our technological civilization is now technically

[9] *Pensées*, v, 508 (Brunschvicg).

capable of annihilating itself. The Promethean age does not get rid of the problems of good and evil, of being and not-being: it strips them of irrelevancies, it isolates them in stark urgency. The elimination by Prometheus of false gods poses the problem of God in all its strictness, leaving only the two alternatives: either nothing and no meaning, or a God who at last can be no other than God.

But Prometheus can repress that tormenting question proper to him and lose his real self in pragmatism, the cult of usefulness, or in materialism, the cult of security. Such is the Prometheus bound our contemporary civilization often displays to us. Marxist society offers us a differently organized and grandiose version of this: political and material construction takes on an absolute value, almost a holiness; the pyramidal hierarchy is more cruelly tyrannical than Pharaoh, and the builder is buried alive in the structure he raises. This is a Prometheus more securely bound. Once again we see that a politically absolute and physical atheism like Marxism, since it totally immerses man in nature and society, destroys the Promethean spirit it pretends theoretically to recognize. Through Marxism Prometheus escapes Prometheus and the ultimate choice between absurdity and meaning. The sham Prometheanism of Marxism is in flight before God and before true atheism; it invents a pagan religion to defend itself against both, and so betrays the spirit of modern times.

Magic done away with, labour would be alone in the world, if it did not itself consecrate the world, if it did not carry on the work of the creation, if it were not capable of fulfilment in the love of men and of God. A civilization based on labour offers tremendous possibilities to humanism and to worship. The Promethean spirit, with all its dangers, inspired the hand which chipped the first flint to make something which was—for everything human is thus ambiguous—at once a tool and a weapon. To call that civilization Babel, to deny its strength and worth, would be to deny man. Evolution is irreversible, and after all, it is by no means certain that even if mankind

could return as a whole to some patriarchal and pastoral
state, the affairs of the spirit would be any better understood or
managed: the shepherd can as easily become a magician and
astrologer as the artisan a materialist atheist. The experience
of Prometheus, which purifies the meaning of the holy, is an
essential step in the journey of man towards God; for, delivered
by that experience from the terrors and from the consolations of
magic, mankind can now know that unrest of the spirit which is
truly an approach to the one God.

THE TIME FOR ACTION AND THE TIME FOR SUFFERING

That philosophical reflection sets up two kinds of atheism is
confirmed in the actual development of history and in the
crisis of our own time. Atheism can only become a social
principle on condition that it fails to keep itself true but falls
back towards the archaism of the closed city-state, by giving
new life and strength to those mythologies and tyrannies which
the knowledge of God had done away with or condemned.
Matter or nature, history or society become, in a truly poly-
theistic muddle, so many substitutes for God, so many un-
realities to take refuge in: they are artificially puffed up, which
conceals the complete collapse of wisdom. Totalitarianism is
the true form, historically and philosophically, of that atheism
which is too ashamed of itself to go all the way, but covers the
panic within by loudly professing in words and deeds a quasi-
scientific and totalitarian fanaticism. The other kind of
atheism, which we have called true or integral atheism,
cannot be actualized in society or become a historical force.
That atheist rebellion which does not replace God with an
ancient idol discovers around itself only the absurdity of a
world deprived of unity and purpose. Such a rebellion can
only end, to start from its worst fate and work up, in private
despair and political aimlessness, or in the compensations of
art, which ideally can charm away its impotence and sterility, or,

lastly, in a moral imperative more sublime than beautiful, but in reality an empty and pointless heroism. Such atheism must be forbidden in a totalitarian society; it could be tolerated in a pluralist culture; but it could never inspire its own positive action, never create a civilization of its own. The times we live in show us more clearly than ever before the two contradictory faces of atheism, political absolutism and moral absolutism.

We hope that we have now shown that this modern age need not necessarily develop towards atheism. If anti-modernist pessimists were right, faith in God ought to prove all modern values illusory, and believers would be obliged to put the clock back so as to overcome the historical and sociological causes of atheism. Now in modern times, even through the hesitant ambiguities of anthropocentrism, man has been developing and growing. To disparage this growth and development would be poor evidence for God as creator of man, who made time and directs history in order that in it something positive may grow and mature and be accomplished. This secular world, this desecrated, pluralist, scientific, technological, Promethean world, is progressive in the true and deepest meaning of the word: in relation to this world, the most certain tendencies of which it contradicts, Communism is like a case of regressive evolution. It tries to break the sequence. It is reactionary. The dynamism of our age, for whoever can understand it properly, is moving towards a critical point for man, is formulating the great question of God. Science and technology underline, in the same way and at the same time, man's roots in the natural world and his emergence from that world. They illuminate sharply both what there is in man that is objective, knowable, open to action from without, and also what is subjective, secret, free and inalienable. Scientific knowledge exasperates almost to breaking point the tensions which *are* man, but it can neither reconcile nor bring to peace what it has separated and opposed. So much so that modern man, had he only science to use, would not possess the knowledge which is properly his. Nor would he possess the power which is his, which destroys more surely than it builds. His labour constructs and builds by speeding up the breakdown of matter and the expenditure of energy, and by slowing down and using natural movements such as waterfalls. Human ingenuity and power is strained to its limits to split an atom, which it cannot put together again. In the same way, when techniques tend to overrule the mind and heart of man they run the risk of making him a spiritless machine, and this is another way of breaking up and destroying. So any power that grows undirected surrounds itself with a shadow of anxiety. Prometheus is both militant and suffering, and there is no technique for ending the contradiction created by techniques. And lastly, political freedom is developing in the same modern sense. People are no longer content to fall in complacently with the whims of princes and powerful men; whole groups of men, once proletarian or subordinate peoples, claim education and political power for themselves. But the wielding of political autonomy is as two-edged as the autonomous use of science or technology. Newly independent communities produce new relationships of dependence which can become as bad as slavery. The dictatorship of the majority dehumanizes man, and all masses, once set free, find it hard to avoid the danger of being both tyrannical and tyrannized. The modern age is a time of action, often of fanatical action: and it is a time of suffering, sometimes of torture. Or rather, there is no real modern age, but we should call modern that development of civilization by which man, realizing his own nature, goes on growing in division and separation, a creature of the heights threatened by the abyss. The times are modern to the extent that they move towards a lucidity which is sharper than before, but beset by bewilderment and anxiety.

And it is a fundamental anxiety, an absolute unrest. As time goes on the reasons for denying and the reasons for believing both become stronger and more pressing. When civilization and Christendom were the same thing it was socially impossible not to believe: from this, faith both profited and suffered. In a secular, tolerant and free society, belief cannot avoid public argument with unbelief. It is wounded, but more free; disarmed, but purified by the break with some political connections. To look at it more profoundly, in these times when man is brought to the point where he can only assert anything by doubting himself, there are three possibilities. First, to run away from the anxiety, to escape from the bewilderment, and take refuge in a kind of paganism, making a whole system of knowledge out of some earthly and historical religion. Second, to accept anxiety as an end-state and try to save the honour of humanity in a meaningless world of chance. And third, to recognize in the living God the holy Being capable of consecrating and giving meaning to man's action and to man's suffering; to confess the Creator, Spirit of our spirit, who unceasingly tests and strengthens his creature, man, in order to awaken in him the desire and the need for salvation, which he can thus conceive, but which he is utterly incapable of attaining by his own resources.

It is true that the modern age has brought to the surface and made more urgent the first two possibilities, of paganism and of true or integral atheism, already implicit in all which in man is heavy, dark and negative. But it is no less true that the spirit of these times, properly understood, and modern values conscientiously lived, though they do not make the paths of human faith and the approaches to God any less steep, do genuinely clear the ground.

Any Christian who curses modern times and accuses them of having killed God and brought agony upon man, is much mistaken. True, the future is wrapped in mystery, and the tensions of our time might end in an apocalyptic explosion. But the expectation of a third, progressive stage growing out of the ruin of modern times is nothing but a romantic illusion or culpable pessimism. Mankind may disappear altogether; if not, it can slip back towards paganism or can go on forward, but only by ever improving in modernity. The Christian was and must remain the first modern man, because it is Christianity which gives impetus to the movement and renewal of history; because faith in a transcendent and immanent God has desecrated nature, secularized society and set man in his true place again, as Promethean lord and consecrator of the world, participating in and obeying its Principle; and lastly because the greatest intensity, the most unfathomable depth of holiness is found in that mystery which joins man's state to the divinity, the solution of the problem of theocentrism or anthropocentrism, for both are true together in the Incarnation of the Word. Christians can therefore carry on the fight against atheism having full faith in that modern age of which they are the pioneers and the first citizens. The Judaeo-Christian tradition, modern by birth, is always threatened by a paganism which is the old age of the world: better than any law of three stages this conflict enables one to understand what underlies history. Such is the first aspect, that more easily seen, of the struggle: we have now described it sufficiently. There is a second, more hidden side to this fight, when faith stripped bare faces integral atheism: in the last chapter we shall try to outline and describe this conflict, if not completely to settle it.

CHAPTER IV

THE SUFFERINGS OF FAITH

THE PROPHETIC SPIRIT

Atheism is a scandal both for reason and for faith. Atheism is necessary for the advancement of reason and the deepening of faith. We should not see in the first of these two propositions only a sweeping fanaticism, for atheism is really and truly madness. It has long been repudiated by all that is wise in the mind and heart of man. Nor should we read into the second a spiritually lazy tolerance of the most pernicious of errors: without the challenge and the criticism and the anxiety which are or call themselves atheist, knowledge of the absolute and experience of the holy would run a grave risk of going astray, of losing their savour, of being corrupted. In dealing with atheism, Christian philosophy cannot seek any compromise whatever between a severity and a leniency both seeming equally excessive. In this field, any indifference or mistaken moderation must be quite out of the question. Atheism can only be understood, in terms of reason and of religion, if both ideas are held together in all their strictness: the scandal and the necessity of atheism.

Catholic tradition allows of no doubt. Ever since the Apostle Paul wrote to the Romans the most terrible indictment of paganism of them all, doctors of the Church, councils and Roman pontiffs have condemned that spiritual defeatism which would make the existence of God a doubtful matter, between the possible and the improbable. The world, or rather the world with man in it, is a sufficient witness to an absolute inaccessible in its essence, indubitable in its existence. To discover in the beings of the world the immanent presence and the infinite transcendence of Being, or to understand the meaning of that activity which works right through the world and so points to something beyond the world, man's mind has no need of the help of revelation or the illumination of grace. These traditional assertions do not mean that God is immediately evident or that his existence is mathematically demonstrable; nor that man is clever enough to discover, by his own skill and his own resources, the key to the riddle of the universe. For to be certain of the existence of God is to confess to a mystery, since that certainty comes not from a logical reconstruction of the system of the world but from the recognition of a radical incompleteness in all that we perceive of what is visible and all that we feel of what is invisible. Man's initiative can never outstrip the prevenient grace of God: when the spirit enters on the road to knowledge of God, it is always God who first manifests himself to the spirit by the spirit. And so, over and above the difference of order between them, natural and super-natural revelation have sufficient in common, enough that is comparable, for the "God of the philosophers and the scientists" to hint at something of the God of Abraham, Isaac and Jacob.

Christianity is not one religion among others, which is to be purified and developed and completed. It is the good news of salvation, the revelation of God to men, the real presence of God among men, it is participation in the life of God while still in this world, offered to all men. So atheism is seen to be doubly scandalous, since the God who is rejected by man's free decision is the God of reason as well as the God of grace. It is just as though the natural and the supernatural self-revelation of God is blocked by man's will not to see and not to know, which thus becomes as hard to understand as to tolerate. How can Christianity resign itself to the frustration of God?

Reason is tested by atheism, but because of atheism faith must suffer.

An explanation can be suggested which reassures reason and consoles faith. The tree of humanity may be alive by the sap of the divinity, but it bears and must bear until the end of time a certain number of dead branches. Error is the natural consequence of sin, and the habit of sinning could explain the stubbornness of many in their ignorance of God. Pride of heart, the desire for mastery, longing for pleasure, these are so many waves of that tide which makes the heart of man a rudderless boat tossed about in mockery. God is above all the absolute demanded by morality, which if it is known and obeyed rescues a man's life from the domination of pride and the tyranny of the flesh. To deny the existence of God is quite calmly to set free the powers of unholy desires and of an unrestrained will. "If God does not exist, anything is allowed", said Dostoevsky's hero: hence the desire that God should not exist, so that all may be allowed, and the reason enslaved, thus submits to the commands of desire so as to make a system of the world which excludes the supreme spoil-sport. The conviction that God does not exist thus resembles the magic ring in Plato's story, the symbol of omnipotence, which made the Lydian shepherd Gyges invisible at will and so enabled him, all restraints thus removed, to flit from pleasure to pleasure, from wrongdoing to wrongdoing. If atheism is thus reduced to a deliberate choosing to reject absolute Good, a choice capable of blinding the understanding by turning the will from its proper end, then the scandal of atheism will be removed, or rather, reduced to the mystery of evil, which, it is traditionally asserted, was introduced into the world by the rebellion of free will against God.

Of such an interpretation of atheism we should certainly retain this, that God reveals himself naturally not to the naked, simple and impersonal reason, but to that depth of personality which is at once the understanding and the will; so that the clarity of a man's perception depends directly on the purity of his heart. There is indeed a kind of atheism which is a possibly unsuccessful attempt to carry immorality to its absolute limits. But this kind of atheism, which one might have called popular had not Don Juan raised it to the aristocratic level, is neither the whole of atheism nor its most profound form. It sometimes happens that a believer not far advanced in spiritual matters, who is overburdened with ritual observances and trammelled by moral obligations, ungenerously attributes to the atheist his own subconscious resentment against a yoke and a burden which he has not been able to lighten by giving himself up to love. Hence arises a complex of lively detestation and unconfessed envy which makes atheism out to be a compensatory myth with no objective truth in it. But really the two kinds of atheism distinguished earlier can neither of them be reduced to a revolt against morality. Political or natural absolutism make the State or Nature the rule above all rules, of absolute compulsion. Moral absolutism, far from wanting to abolish conscience by rejecting God, makes the categorical imperative an objection to the existence of a God who, if he existed, could not tolerate evil, being by definition able to suppress it. Finally, to explain away atheism as due to an evil will is to set oneself up in God's place, arrogating to oneself the right to probe into men's hearts and consciences; it is to refuse *a priori* to seek the causes of atheism in the failings of believers who have been able, by their own faults, to compromise the cause of God. Accusing others can be only a cover for the most Pharisaic self-justification.

There is another interpretation of atheism, diametrically opposed to that we have just rejected, which is inspired by what we might call a prophetic spirit: in order to rediscover the living God, such an interpretation accuses God's people. Atheism is said to be the result of and the penalty for the sins against the spirit committed by those chosen to be witnesses, who instead of putting themselves at God's service used God in their own, in order to improve their place in the world and to protect by abuse of religion the privileges and esteem they enjoyed merely through power or worldly self-aggrandizement. Was not the first thing the faith suffered less attack from atheists than degradation by believers to the level of a mark of aristocratic distinction, a guarantee valid for this world and the next? Such men made faith knowledge, culture, art—they paganized the God of Moses and of Christ. The tremendous spread of contemporary atheism would thus be a sign of the just judgement of God on the dulling and hardening and rotting of faith, the ill-kept secret of centuries ostensibly Christian. A truly Biblical or evangelical understanding of atheism will therefore not be found among the preachers of crusades against the godless, who are really politicians, nor among orthodox intellectuals, amateurs engaged in academic argument over atheist philosophies, who are so anxious to understand them and to pick out the fragments or great chunks of truth they contain. It is to be found among the new prophets who reawaken the feeling for God with great outbursts of wrath from within or from outside of churches dozing with easy consciences. Believers who are conventional conformists thus find themselves stigmatized as more atheist than the atheists; they claim to have faith, but are careful of the conversion of their hearts. Reformed Christianity, which gives such great and proper importance in its spiritual life to the remembrance of the prophets of Israel, inclines to such an interpretation of atheism. The worker-priests, too, in contemporary Catholicism, share this prophetic spirit: having come to grips with atheism, these missionaries carry their witness in a profoundly new way into the heart of the dechristianized masses, breaking away altogether from middle-class society and refusing with a courage that is perhaps rashness the protection of the older forms of Christianity.

The minds of men—even of Christian men—in this world lapse so easily into carnality and paganism that no prophet is ever completely wrong. There is in such a prophetic interpretation of contemporary atheism a challenge and a summons a believer cannot contrive to escape. In the Judaeo-Christian tradi-

tion and especially since the Incarnation, God is completely
involved in the people he chose, and the faithlessness of the
faithful could therefore produce a detestable travesty of God.
Wars of religion, which were really and fundamentally political, debased the faith until it became one with a narrow
nationalism. God was numbered among the supporters of the
established powers and the ruling classes, he was used to keep
the crowd of the lowly and the weak resigned to injustice. The
claim for social and socialist justice made by a Marx or a
Proudhon could therefore plausibly put together the hope for
liberation and the rejection of God. To consider it more
generally and more profoundly, if atheism has glorified the
earth and civic virtue as against God, this is because too
many Christians, contaminated by what looks like Platonism
but is really Manicheism, have seen in the temporal
and social condition of man only an accidental misfortune, a
consequence of sin; setting the Redeemer against the Creator,
they have made his world only a half-real place of passage,
a testing-ground. We must certainly not fail to denounce in
Marxism a pagan perversion of Christianity; but only on
condition that we remember that those Christian truths which
atheism ridicules have first been misunderstood and travestied
by the believers who had them in their keeping. True, Marx's
proletariat, which takes upon itself the evil of the world, that
is, man's exploitation of man, descends to the depths of
the hell of inhumanity in order eventually to deliver humanity
from its essential evil in a society of brothers on a renovated
earth; this proletariat-saviour is, as has been said often
enough, a literal transposition into other terms of the God-Man
who by his suffering sets man free from sin and works for the
Kingdom to come. But Marx could only arise as a prophet of
error, a misleading guide, because Christendom was not
worthy enough to produce inspired prophets who could denounce what was intolerable in the condition of the proletariat
or—for it is the same problem—in colonial subservience. Or
rather, Christians who did understand and act, and saved

something more than their own honour, arose too late to prevent the revolution against humiliation and slavery that was bound to come from giving a great impetus to atheist philosophy and atheist political theory. To forget that the God of the prophets and of the saints is first and foremost the God of divine wrath against all forms of iniquity is a form of practical atheism. And atheism attracts and begets atheism.

But this prophetic spirit also can go wrong and spoil: it can become a blind ideology and lose itself in what can be called, pejoratively, "propheticism". Then, Christendom is confused with the Church, and the Christian world becomes the result of the victory of the world over Christianity; faith is then considered, because of its unavoidable psychological and sociological lapse, to be such that it can no longer be distinguished from debatable opinion or behaviour which is open to question. Then this despair stirs up an apocalyptic hope: why should not philosophical and political atheism be the instrument of a vast and providential purification? Communism thinks itself called to destroy all religion, but wherever it spreads it only clears away such intellectual or social structures as over-burden and paralyse and falsify faith. God is not killed when a bourgeois, capitalist and basically materialist society is swept from the pages of history: such a society only identified its own cause and God's to escape the judgement of God. This sort of "propheticism" follows with a literalness which is almost servile the prophets of Israel, who risked being thought defeatists because they considered the Assyrians to be the instrument of divine wrath against the prevarications of God's chosen people. According to this view, atheism is the actualization of the prophetic spirit itself, having become an irresistible historical force in Communism and having reached the highest point of philosophical criticism. By destroying Pharisaic societies which make use of God in their practical misrepresentations of him, and which thus entomb the living God, atheism becomes—but only after a seemingly endless night of purification—the means, immediately terrifying but in the long run beneficial, used by Providence to prepare for an unimaginable resurrection of God in a world which is wholly new.

Taken to such extremes, the idea of atheism as a purifier becomes really indefensible, and propheticism is only a vicious caricature of the prophetic spirit. The mistake is to make a false historical comparison. Communism is not a youthful barbarism, rough and undeveloped, bringing fresh blood into history, breaking up and revivifying an empire grown greedy and old and tired. It is a complete social organization, a whole system of man and the world, which confines man to this world, not even admitting an unknowable as a possible hypothesis; as we have shown sufficiently already, it puts modern techniques at the service of a movement that is retrograde politically, intellectually and spiritually. The apocalyptic propheticism we have described was adopted by or won the sympathy of some Christians after the last war. They were over-eager for improvement and willing to buy it at the highest price. But they despaired too soon of a modern, liberal, democratic society, Christian in spirit, which had often, it is true, been unworthy of its own spirit, but which had hardly begun its work in the world and certainly did not deserve to perish. And it was surely tempting Providence to expect that everything would be set right by the catastrophic purification of Communism becoming universally active. Communism has not in fact won over the majority of mankind: it treats man, and man's irrepressible need for freedom, too badly not to be doomed to defeat itself from within. Communism's welding together of atheist ideology and a totalitarian society runs counter both to human progress and to the movement of history. No propheticism could justify such bad politics. The devil may well assist in the work of God in some mysterious way which will only be clear at the end of all things; but this does not give men the right to collaborate with the devil under the pretext of dialectically advancing God's affairs.

The two statements at the beginning of this chapter, that

atheism is a scandal and that it is necessary, cannot then be separated, despite their apparent contrariety. To choose between them, to exclude one and assume the truth of the other, is to be mistaken about atheism and to compromise faith. It is extremely difficult to fight sternly against atheism as an evil which introduces a lethal poison into the spirit and into society, and at the same time to understand that atheism's denial can have a deepening and purifying effect on faith. We have just seen that to sacrifice one of these requirements to the other leads either to Pharisaism or to propheticism.

The fact that propheticism is wrong does not mean that resistance to and understanding of atheism do not need the help of the prophetic spirit. Moses, the heroic pioneer of monotheism, was the first and perhaps the greatest of the prophets, and whenever reason or faith find God, Moses is explicitly or implicitly commemorated. In the search for God by our natural powers there is no means which cannot also become an obstacle: such is this world, bearing clear evidence of its contingency yet so easily usurping the place of the absolute; such too is the spirit of man, who knows with certainty that he is obsessed by the idea of the infinite, yet no sooner realizes this than he breaks his upward flight too soon, and takes himself, not without some plausibility, to be his only source and first principle. The vigilance of the prophet is therefore needed to prevent a lapse into idolatry. Where prophets are wanting, polytheism and pantheism, the gods and Fate, swiftly cover up the natural knowledge of God until it becomes unrecognizable for what it is. The prophetic spirit is thus the aspect of truth in the atheist denial which so efficiently shatters images and likenesses of God which are not God.

The prophet is besides absolutely intolerant of injustice; and the prophetic spirit, although it is sometimes difficult to see that it is so, is a function of the Church. This intolerance is not only a moral attitude but is metaphysical and religious, and ensures correctness of vision and authenticity of belief. In this world, evil is not only a strong objection to the existence of God but also, if it can be expressed in this way, an a-theist fact, a test for reason and suffering for faith; for evil, since it is sin, is God-less, apart from God, disowned by God. Witness to God is therefore only trustworthy when it is thought and lived in a prophetic spirit in a fight which is both public and private against all forms of evil. One of the classic functions of the prophet is to confound believers who, under the specious name of resignation, give in to great political and social injustice, and so add their contribution to atheism; they are really responsible for the death of God in men's hearts and in society. The prophetic spirit arms reason and faith against the political and natural absolutism of totalitarian atheism: because of it reason and faith know that the spirit of Babel can purify neither reason nor faith. And lastly, when it is a matter of facing up to the most rigorous and shattering atheism of all, the essence of which is moral absolutism and which causes faith the greatest suffering, the prophetic spirit is a useful support, an indispensable ally. But before we consider this last battle, it may be a good thing to look more closely at an actual case, and a very great one.

THE NEED TO REDISCOVER PASCAL

No one was ever more concerned about atheism than Pascal: it horrified him but also strangely and strongly attracted him. The substance of Pascal's genius was in the will to conquer atheism while also understanding its lesson. In Pascal we have the ideal form of polemics and dialogue used together, and of a kind of thinking which treats its opponent, without compromise, as a sort of partner in the discussion, using the dialectics of atheism to purify and deepen faith. Pascal is our contemporary, a more powerful ally against today's atheism than against the free-thinking unbelief of the seventeenth century, a lesser form, a sort of mock-up, of the most true and genuine atheism. And nothing throws more light on our problem than an application of the famous *Conversations with M. de Saci*.

In Pascal's time as in our own, unbelief was a house divided against itself: it appealed sometimes to a kind of Stoicism then revived and much in vogue, and sometimes to Montaigne, whose growing influence was very alarming to the Church. Pascal explains to M. de Saci, whose Jansenism considered it culpable curiosity to try to find out ideas so dangerous to the faith, how the great contradictory errors of Epictetus and Montaigne are partial truths, perverted and falsified, which obstinate narrow-mindedness treats as mutually exclusive, but which can all be used and understood in a Christian philosophy so as to be preserved together and reconciled. Epictetus was conscious of the greatness of man and thought him capable of attaining by his own powers alone to complete freedom and complete wisdom; for that, it is necessary, but also sufficient, that man should consider himself as part of the world and should cleave with all his mind to divine necessity which makes the world solid, rational, mightily and luminously existent. Montaigne was very sharply aware of man's wretchedness, and thought to have found its source in his utter powerlessness, from which derived his spiritual need to find a haven in affirmation, in assurance, in certainty. Hence arose a restless doubt, the dizzy circle of a denial endlessly denying itself, an ever-frustrated conscience and a human nature devoid of content which could fill itself only by self-deception, by the pretence of permanence in a contingent and precarious society. Epictetus exaggerated man's legitimate self-respect into arrogant pride and haughtiness. Montaigne deepened to despair the wretchedness of a mind which is by its nature cut off from the absolute. Each of these two thinkers was too much aware of half of man to be able to conceive of the whole; each one's premise was right, but his deductions from it were false because he did not know or misunderstood the other's. Dialectical knowledge of man as at one and the same time great and wretched cannot be achieved except in a Christian philosophy, which preserves the truths of both Epictetus and Montaigne.

In *Conversations with M. de Saci*, literally interpreted,

Pascal does not actually argue against atheism. The Stoics did not deny God's existence: they identified him with nature. And if Montaigne doomed reason to agnosticism, it was so that he might argue the better against atheists who said more about it than they knew, and save faith by fideism. Yet Pascal's bringing together of the Stoics and Montaigne astonishingly foreshadows the arguments between the forms of contemporary atheism.

So, Marxist Hegelianism plays the part taken by the neo-Stoicism used and judged by Pascal. The outlines are the same, but larger, more firmly drawn and with a clearer design than in his book. It is no longer man as an individual who is asked to reject his solitude by cleaving to the solidarity of the whole, but man as a collective unity; by only tackling problems which are in fact solved man can attain to complete wisdom in building a classless society which will give point and meaning to history, which thus becomes consistent, coherent and understandable from beginning to end. Man's pride is exalted into the atheist's rejection of transcendence and mystery, and the totality in process of self-achievement which history has become is really the God invented by atheism to cut God out completely.

Pascal's Montaigne is, by a sort of divination, nearer to modern existentialists than to the Montaigne of the *Essays*: this opinion which cannot be expressed by any affirmative term, this equivalence of contraries, this empty nothingness of the life within, this despairing power of negation which makes impossible or false any affirmation of being—such a description is a more exact summary of Sartre's thought than of Montaigne's philosophy, which is far more various and many-sided. To the Stoic or Hegelian world, which is a continuum and anything but temporary or surpassable, to their idea of fate or history which is or is being actualized, setting man free by demanding of him the ultimate consent of his whole thought and action, are opposed a fragmented world so contingent as to be meaningless, and a forlorn freedom condemned to say "No", which no power, not even divine, could grasp or understand; a human existence with no essence, which is at each moment whatever it makes itself. Such are Montaigne's doubts, as rethought and carried to extremes by Pascal, who thus makes them similar in principle and in spirit to the most thoroughgoing form of contemporary atheism.

As we have shown, and as Pascal confirms, the atheism of individual solitude and that of collective solidarity, once they are brought together, cannot but destroy one another, even if, to use them as symbols, Montaigne is more powerful against Epictetus than Epictetus against Montaigne. Pascal put the real problem rightly: can a Christian exegesis of the two forms of atheism save them from mutual contradiction and destruction by the fine understanding and charity of the *Conversations*?

Marxist Hegelianism shows that man cannot deny God without using the idea of God, wholly projected into the world, or rather, more precisely, into an immanence in the world which excludes transcendence and mystery. God is the unity of the real, the rational and the ideal: and the world, in which all that is real is already rational and all that is rational will one day be real; and history, in which, as it continually improves, the gap between what is done and what ought to be done progressively narrows until it closes, and in which existence increases its value and value increases its existence; these two, the world and history, are nothing other than God in the process of actualizing himself. Marxist man, because he understands the world and works with history, is therefore capable of attaining to a wisdom indistinguishable from salvation, thanks to which, by being in harmony with others and with the whole of reality, he is in harmony with himself. This is a wisdom, a salvation, which comes willy-nilly through God, for it supposes that the world and man in the world make an absolute understandable in itself and justified by itself. But it is a wisdom, a salvation, that is terribly vulnerable, for a mere grain of

existentialist thought is enough to shatter to pieces this doubtful, contradictory and abstract God; or, more generally, to
shatter any pantheist system, and consequently Marxist
Hegelianism, just as Montaigne only needed a pinch of irony
to reduce to powder the pride of the Stoics. A Christian philosopher, especially one inspired by Pascal, can treat Marxist
atheism more considerately, for he can find in it the important
and instructive check one must encounter who seeks God without knowing he is doing so. It is basically not atheism at all,
for it cannot be believed in or put into practice except by bringing down to earth and putting to work belief in God, aspiration
towards wisdom, and expectation of salvation, all of which it
thus proves to be natural to man or, to use the term in a
different sense, all of which it tries in vain to prove completely
natural. This belief, aspiration and expectation cannot be
rooted out; Marxist atheism, far from eradicating them, turns
them away from their true end while trying to take over and
use their strength and power.

For Marxism, existentialist atheism is socially pathological.
But a contemporary Pascal would not share this harsh mis-
judgement. The existentialist atheist, like the Hegelian atheist,
cannot dispense with the idea of God. He knows, taking his
philosophical penetration much deeper than Marxism, that in
that idea should be united the supreme reality and the perfection of value. He then adds that this would make up a contradiction, for both by definition and experience existence is
that which has no value and value is that which cannot exist.
Hence the sophistical conclusion that God is impossible.
But the existentialist has really only shown that a world in
which there is a tension between what is done and what ought to
be done, where there is permanent strife between ideal and
reality, where value is always a demand within or beyond
existence, such a world should not be confused with God,
nor with the Kingdom of God visible to the eyes and evident
to the spirit. This is a refutation of any pantheism. This is useful
to Christian philosophy, but more precious still is the sense of

the silence or the absence of God which is the foundation of existentialist *Angst*, or unrest. With excessively dogmatic awkwardness this is made a proof of the non-existence of God; but it is easy to see that it is at once an exaggeration and a debasement of the unrest of the religious mind. Man's heart, as St Augustine practically said, cannot find peace until he finds an infinite being who is infinitely good, and an infinite good which is supremely existent; and he will not find what he seeks in temporal or natural things, even if he could with his intelligence and his longing exhaust their substance and their value.

So these two forms of atheism can only be truly understood if we start from that free search for God which is the life of all life and the spirit of all spirit. On the one hand, God is found too quickly and too cheaply by being actualized in nature and in history, in a pagan manner; life is sterilized, the spirit is violated, for living and thinking men are imprisoned in what Teilhard de Chardin has profoundly called "terrenism". On the other hand, God is judged impossible to find, because the world presents the sight, the ultimately unbearable sight— and these are Sartre's very words—of an "aborted God": and it is admitted that conscience frustrated in its search for God is for ever unhappy because its need for an absolute is absolutely betrayed. A Christian philosopher could, by re-discovering Pascal, preserve the principles and the vigour of the two forms of atheism while completely rejecting conclusions which condemn man to do without the true God. The high hope of a humanity reconciled in a world renewed, and despair at the sufferings of the Good and the One in this world of pretence and of separation, of grief and sin, these two feelings are inseparable from faith in the true God made alive by the prophets. Nothing of positive value in Marxism or in existentialism is lost, while all that is negative in them is ruthlessly cut out. Pascal showed well enough that Christian faith could take up the strength of atheism of whatever form in such a way that "all can find there more than they desire", for example by joining together by going beyond them "those who could not come together at their infinitely lower level".[1]

THE TRIAL IN THE WILDERNESS

If a well-ordered Christian philosophy can purify atheist thought, atheism itself can purify faith through suffering. From now on we shall no longer deal with systems hostile to God and doomed to an unending hostility to one another; only recourse to God can end that hostility, but that they reject, without being able to get rid of a problem the spirit is bound by its nature to face. We shall now consider atheism's sharpest cutting edge: why is faith fundamentally so vulnerable to its stroke, even though, if it is inspired as it should be, it remains fearlessly certain of itself?

In the same way as the prophets, iconoclastic as they were, atheism's denial is valid first of all against anthropocentrism and polytheism of all kinds. Ironic criticism of mythology, righteous anger against idolatry, impious refusal to make superficial sacrifices to the gods—these are so many acts condemned at one time or another as irreligious, which yet made straight the ways of the one Lord. Witnesses to the unknown God and Christ's disciples suffered torture and death for the crime of atheism. Athens made Socrates drink the hemlock because, if we can believe Plato, he honoured the gods of the city less than the *daimon* appointed to him and the Idea of the Good which illuminates all men's minds. Before that, Anaxagoras—Socrates had been awakened to philosophy by an inspired saying of his, monotheist even so early—had had to go into exile to save his life, threatened by the charge of atheism. For that discoverer of the world of the spirit was also a physical scientist who believed the moon to be a stone and not a god. In the age of the persecutions, the first of the Christian apologists claimed this same accusation of atheism, which doomed the worshippers of the true God to capital

[1] Pascal, *op. cit.*, p. 161 (Brunschvicg).

punishment, as a glorious title: "They call us atheists," cried Justin Martyr,[2] "and we admit to being atheists so far as such so-called gods are concerned."

Ancient history? By no means; for the world, ancient or modern, for ever throws up gods with regard to which Christians must be called atheists. In a sense, mythology and paganism do belong to man's past, but this past is kept in check rather than abolished. It comes back, more or less disguised, seducing the heart, charming the imagination, conquering the mind. To think that the gods died in the twilight of the old mythology is a foolish illusion, which the gods take advantage of in order to live longer still. And no doubt it will need the blast and blaze of the Last Judgement to convince all men fully and finally of the vanity of the gods they never stopped believing in. Man is so profoundly religious by nature that he is unable not to make religions for himself, of his will to power, of his desires and his values, and this begets many gods, today as always. Polytheism is not just the religion of early man: it has its origin in the corruption of real religious feelings. It could be stated as a rule, that man becomes polytheist whenever, since he cannot abdicate from his reason, he thinks carnally according to worldly ideas. And atheism is a valid attack on polytheism.

Sociological theories of religion are good explanations and successfully destructive of any nationalist polytheism, any religion of a closed community. There are some gods of whom Lachelier said, to show them false, that they are born in the streets, the product of collective excitement. Class, nation, race, empire—every group of men setting itself up in opposition to some other group, challenging its right to exist, makes a carnal religion of its fanatical patriotism, and slips into believing that in reducing its enemy to despair, slavery or death it is executing the judgement of its gods, or of one God, who is then a pagan god. War, so long as there are men who fight one another, is Manicheist and polytheist, and especially when it is a crusade, a holy war, a revolutionary war; it even insinuates

[2] Justin Martyr, *First Apology*, VI, 1.

paganism within such highly spiritual religions as Islam and Christianity. Even if the war is just, paganism is still an imminent danger. How could a man accept the risk to his own life or take another's unless the Absolute were concerned to absolve his violence and consecrate his sacrifice? Yet his enemy consoles himself with the same sublime thoughts. So God is divided against himself and the Absolute is split: this split and this division are used by atheism, justly against the gods, but vainly against God. If war were the last word of history and the whole destiny of man, polytheism would be right, and the Old Testament prophets would have been serving the great revelation of monotheism faithfully and exactly when they announced the final victory of the Spirit of God over war.

The number of mutually aggressive communities is a permanent source of polytheism, but so also is the diversity of men's desires and the disparity of their strength: the greatness, the spread, of this diversity and this disparity are shocking, but the shock is deliberately ignored. There is one such polytheism easy to expose: that of Don Juan, who dissipates his passion in the great number of his desires, who tries to make each instant absolute, each fleeting adventure an eternity sufficient to itself. To push the fragmentation of the absolute to such extremes is a way of denying God and of profaning religion which can reach a Satanic greatness. Don Juan represents a limit which is scarely attainable; but such polytheism, in forms sometimes strictly removed from any libertinism, is a possibility for man, pulled this way and that by friendships and loves, duties and pleasures, goods and values, which cannot easily all be reduced to a unified order. Man then lives in a kind of polytheist state, serving several masters, passing from the worship of one god to that of another. Poetry? No: a phenomenological description, for every human attachment comes from man's limitless freedom and naturally transforms its object into an idol. Now it is part of the illogical nature of polytheism that one idol never interferes with any other idol, one god never harms another: the divinities now temporarily neglected are close by in the shadows, quietly waiting to appear again in the future. Polytheism is very often really atheism, even when it is only lived in practice and never gets as far as being aware of its truest justification; for to believe in many gods is an easy way of rejecting the one God. And that other atheism, which denounces and destroys the fetishes begotten by desires or rapidly shifting values, by psychoanalysing such polytheism, is nearer to faith and its prophetic spirit.

It sometimes happens that polytheism destroys itself, and one of its gods shatters the older pantheon and clothes himself in the spoils of his rivals' attributes; or even that this last god disappears himself and leaves the whole temple to a single Fate, the divine and impersonal truth of man and the world. The coexistence of many values is no longer allowed, for there is only one, and man's life is entirely given up to private piety or public works, to art or science or politics; interest which may be given to some other value will not be really love but recreation in which to gather strength to love the more what alone counts. But polytheism is not really surpassed: for a limited value, puffed up quite falsely into an absolute, is still precarious and finite, and the god thus improperly promoted is still one of the gods. Here we can see the origin of that political absolutism which has become the religion of many of our contemporaries. But no value, even if it contain in itself indefinite capacities for actualization, can be truly absolute so long as it has a sensible shape and a conceptual form. Even truth can be made into an idol, as Pascal said. The absolutism of one value only makes a false monotheism and, instead of representing God, only constructs an abstract Destiny. It can be seen how fanatical devotion to one value, even when it is thought to be religious, misses God and makes itself the slave of fate.

So atheism has not disproved God's existence by correctly psychoanalysing the fanatic and the fatalist. That there is in any value an aspect of precariousness and contingency; that the mind only makes one value absolute because of resentment against others, only fanatically loving beauty, for example, because despairing of truth; that the mind does not escape thus from polytheism and the war of the gods; that values as they are in fact cannot be welded together but remain many and separate; and that to think of the universe as a whole with a single destiny is to preclude all choice, to destroy all meaning by asserting the equivalence of values, and to engulf all things in nothingness; none of these propositions is basically atheist, for they are only valid against misrepresentations themselves empty of God.

Atheism is fundamentally prophetic. There is nothing in the world or in man which cannot signify or symbolize God, for all things are effects and reflections of his causality. But to confuse the thing signified with the sign, the symbol with the reality, this is to introduce plurality into God and to content oneself with the polytheism natural to carnal man, or rather, to man whose spirit is carnal. Multiplicity of beings and plurality of values bear witness to a God as source of those beings and principle of those values, but only provided he is not confused either with one being or with one value, nor indeed confused with a unity immanent in but not existing separately from beings and values; this would destroy what it claims to build, by reducing it to a fatalist system. The real victims of atheism are polytheism and false monotheism.

Yet faith is tested by atheism. For faith is always the faith of a particular man who feels and imagines as well as thinks, and who cannot do without some image or likeness of God; he is always tempted either to reject the world and its values to glorify God alone, or to give to the world and its values a consistence, a necessity and a beauty which are practically divine. Atheism is then painful but profitable to faith, when it makes a man release the catch he thought he held, a too sensible image or a too determinate idea, a systematic attitude of hostility to the world which reduces God to the mere shadow of his own rejection, or an unreflecting and prejudiced assent which ranks the Godhead as obvious along with the appearances of things. But to have a faith which is true and spiritual, we must both use and not use images and likenesses, accept and welcome things as they are and at the same time wish with all our hearts that they were different. When the prophetic spirit uses atheism, it awakens the unrest of the spirit, and it is not the enemy of faith but only a faith asleep. The old gods and Fate, always on the point of reappearing, never cease to threaten belief in God, and in its highest form atheism is a machine for grinding the gods and Fate into dust.

Moses, that great teacher of faith, led the chosen people out of a society too highly organized and took them into the wilderness, far from anywhere friendly to man, so as to shield his people better from the gods and so teach them, in a religion which was neither intellectual nor a cult of nature, the unimaginable nearness and at the same time the utter transcendence of God. The faith he first preached was not a passive one of indifference to the world or self-abandonment to Fate: it was the beginning of a mission which was to cover and to uplift the whole world without ever becoming wholly of the world. So did the prophets purify faith: atheist criticism, even at its most inspired, can never do more than set out a deceptive likeness of their purification. When the model is forgotten, the imitation must remain a sterile mockery.

THE CRISIS OF WISDOM

Although atheism properly and effectively criticizes false and misleading images of God, it cannot therefore conclude that he is dead. Faith knows that God is not a force of nature, nor an absolute monarch whose realm is heaven and earth and whose subjects are angels and men, nor a craftsman who moulded matter in the shape of the world; neither is he an abstract principle which unifies and integrates reality, nor an immanent law of universal organization. True faith rejects equally both idolatry and "ideolatry". A prophetically inspired understanding of atheist criticism would, then, have taken the fuses out of the bombshell of atheism, did there not always subsist that spiritual revolt which simply states, as the metaphysical corollary of an ethical necessity, the impossibility of the existence of God. There indeed, as we have said throughout this essay, is the quintessence of atheism, its sharpest point, its most formidable attack.

First we must stress the *a priori* character of this most profound form of atheism, which is also its original form. The question is not to discover whether or not the world is that "Isle of Mystery", whether or not it is inhabited by the secret, active and kindly genius of some Captain Nemo, to recall Jules Verne's *Twenty Thousand Leagues under the Sea*, in which Claudel saw—perhaps somewhat riskily—a symbolic apologetics. If that were the problem of God, when everywhere had been searched, everything turned over and even the darkest corners explored, we should have to look at the evidence, draw up a statement of failure, after an honestly conducted search, and write the death-certificate of a persistent dream of man: God is dead. The *yes* and *no* were long in the balance, it is true, but now it is settled: we have searched and there is no one there. Captain Nemo does not exist.

Such a tritely positivist atheism misses the point of the problem altogether. Not so that atheism which questions the idea of God as it appears to the purest minds, the absolute Good. Morality, in fact, even if men sometimes see it as a collection of duties not easily reconcilable with one another, is not a value like other values, subject to the same law of competition and argument. It is by its very loftiness taken out of the common run of values; it is less a static image than a dynamic and categorical demand. Raised to absoluteness by an effort of pure thought, it allows faith a precise idea of God.

Common belief calls on the Good Lord; the greatest of metaphysicians recognizes the Idea of the Good (which is not, he adds, an Idea) as the supreme principle of being and of spirit. The most destructive atheist criticism and the most prophetically pure faith are at one in sending packing the gods and all images of God in which there is not found the absolute Good. But atheism, as a form of moral absolutism, even though it keeps the Good as a moral imperative, not only refuses the transition from imperative to existence but by a sort of inverted ontological argument makes, *a priori*, that imperative a reason, which it claims is decisive, for the non-existence of the Good, in a proof which is as it were immediate and almost intuitive.

The world as it is and as it happens imposes on the mind proof of the existence of evil, a web of misdeeds and misfortunes neither compensatable nor redeemable in this world, which is woven by the twin shuttles of nature and history. This evil would not stupefy the heart nor bewilder the mind were there not in man, ineffable, uncontrollable and ineradicable, the idea of absolute Good. The truest atheism is not content merely to agree with this; it claims to draw from it all its irresistible force. If this Good had existence other than merely ideal, if it could have said that "I AM" which Moses heard from the burning bush, evil would at once become a mere appearance and the duty to call it by its proper name and to take it on and fight it, the duty which gives man his dignity, would lose all meaning, for the fight is merely a sham when the enemy is an illusion. How indeed could the Good, if he were absolutely real, support the real existence in the universe of his own contrary, which St Thomas, like Plato before him, calls evil? That would be a metaphysical scandal, for then the absolute would be limited, the power of God fettered; or, what is more serious, an ethical scandal, for it would look as though the Good's policy with regard to evil was less one of resistance than of attenuation or even of collaboration. There are plenty of ingenious and theoretically apposite answers in theodicy which remove one or other of these scandals for the believer. But the strength of atheism's denial is scarcely lessened. Every theodicy appeals, in fact, to God's power and his righteousness, both infinite; even if our necessarily finite experience remains dark and doubtful, the mind arguing this out with itself must learn that these two, the power and righteousness of God, can draw from evil, even that which seems most hopeless, a good which is invisible and mysterious, which will set all things in order, and enable us to dismiss the intolerable thought of any check on omnipotent Goodness. But it must be clearly understood that even a faultless refutation of atheism would also provide it with ground for argument. Theodicy appeals to a divine wisdom as source and explanation of all that is; the idea, if it is natural to the mind, is not specifically Christian. This God who writes straight on crooked lines is also the God of all forms of pantheism (among which are included all Hegelian systems), the God who uses the sufferings, the mistakes and the passions of men to direct history and the world towards their fulfilment, which is immanent in them, the world thus becoming wisdom in action. Because they prove too much, theodicies and philosophies of wisdom are open to the attacks of the most profound kind of atheism, which sees in them a consolatory mythology or a deceitful poetry, and accuses them of suppressing, not resolving, the insoluble problem of evil, from fear of facing it squarely and fully experiencing it.

Atheism in the form of moral absolutism works in the service of faith so far as it declares the death of the God of metaphysical rationalism and optimism, and also so far as it courageously faces the problem of evil. At the level of this form of atheism, the more common forms hardly survive: those, that is, which regard the evil in the world as a defect which can be made good by science and technology. But this same atheism intensifies the suffering of faith by asking whether man, frail and faltering though he is, since he has in himself the idea of the good and utterly condemns evil, is not more divine than God, who, since he justifies by his existence all that is, gives evil a sort of "freedom of the city" in the historical universe of his creation. We can see how this integral atheism can be called a kind of humanism, exalting man by denying God's existence. But at what cost? The greatness it attributes to man is no longer

Promethean, for between an unjustifiable world and man, who possesses the ideas—undeniable, but terrifyingly empty—of meaning, reason and purpose, there is an irreparable division. On the pinnacle of the world is set an unsurmountable absurdity: man, whose greatness lies in his not only looking for meaning but demanding it, yet has himself no meaning. Better still, this atheism which uses irony in its own cause when it suggests that God's only excuse is that he does not exist, yet needs this God, for otherwise its accusation against him is dissipated into nothingness; nor does it always avoid this consequence, that it hurls its abuse and its insults into the silence and the darkness. The comedy of this should humble its proud agony of spirit.

Lastly, atheism breaks in on a proof of God's existence, just as it is reaching its conclusion, by disclosing the necessity, metaphysical and ethical, for the existence of the Good— we may well think this proof the ultimate proof, underlying all others—and then refusing to grant the logicality of the logic, in order to be able to admit with complete honesty the irrefutable existence of evil. The Good ought to exist, but does not: so there is beneath all things only a non-sense worse than non-existence. Let us not think we have refuted integral atheism by giving a general account of it or by completely enumerating its contradictions. For the world is such, for this sort of atheism, that it sets spirit against spirit, and the contradiction is inevitable if the pathos of man's condition is conscientiously faced.

More even than the death of God, integral atheism prosecutes the death of wisdom and of faith, which can shut itself up, in self-defence, within the walls of a rationalist and optimistic system of knowledge, and may risk being buried in the debris of an untenable position. Atheism forbids faith to use God to water down, to take the edge off or dissolve away the agony of evil. Job's comforters, defenders of God and makers of pious theodicies, are properly sent packing by a revolt which can as well be atheist as prophetic. The true believer is the old man Job, who thinks his misfortune incomprehensible and unjust, because he knows for certain that the God he loves does not ask of him the dumb resignation of a slave; he dares to question the Lord directly, because he knows that only God can have the last word in this dramatic trial of reason and power. "Despite all the arguments used by theologians and philosophers since the beginnings of atheism," says Gabriel Marcel, "it finds its permanent refuelling base in the existence of evil and the suffering of the innocent."[3] Not that we need despair entirely of philosophy and theology: but both of them ought to take back and work over again too many brief and peremptory answers which cannot quieten man's unrest in the face of evil, and which only inject, as Marcel might say, more fuel into the atheist system. We have to grant our opponent that evil permanently provokes man to atheism. Misfortune and injustice, death and the works of death, by their perennial insolence and their unchecked proliferation, make God seem improbable. Yet if evil cannot be explained and absolved by reason or by mystery, there cannot be any other issue for the adventure of man than a nihilist despair that is the suicide of the mind. Evil both denies God and awakens the need for God; in evil, reasons for denying and reasons for believing are mingled, and like wrestlers twined together and holding each other immobile for a moment, seem to balance their strengths and hold each other up, but in the end the equilibrium will be broken so far as faith shows itself as critical of conventional theodicies as atheism, if it can endure to the end the passion it suffers through evil, and so overcome atheism by a better understanding of the pathos of man's condition. Evil, as we have already said, is *a-theist* in the proper sense, and victory over atheism could only be ensured by the absolution of evil and the redemption of the world; for what is so bewildering for the mind as it faces the problem of evil is less the general emotional confusion it engenders than the clear agony of the intellect produced by its seeing in evil the absence or the

[3] In *L'athéisme contemporain*, Ed. Fides Givini, 1956, p. 90.

silence of God, of whose existence it has such a deeply-rooted certitude.

So faith is purified by suffering. The God whose existence is questioned by painful reflection on the problem of evil is not the same as the architect of the universe or the spirit of history, that great idol called by Maritain "the preposterous Emperor of the World". God is not a Captain Nemo whose kindly spirit will come to the assistance of those shipwrecked in the storms of life, miraculously extricating them from their difficulties when they become dangerous. That fake island is a ridiculous parody of the mystery of this world. The miracles God performs, even if they draw the veil aside for a fleeting moment, remain enveloped in clouds of mystery, and do not excuse men from suffering evil and fighting against it, which passion and action define the state and duty of man and, according to the prophets, painfully and arduously goad and stimulate belief in God. Non-resignation to injustice is one of the essential characteristics of the prophetic spirit, and it is both service and knowledge of God. It was to a people freed from the evil of their slavery by their decision to break with established disorder that Moses was able to teach again the faith of their fathers. Because evil denies God, religious feeling is only true and valid if it forces itself to deny evil in order to find God by harmonizing itself with the absolute Good.

It is thus the prophetic spirit rather than atheism which is the salt which preserves belief in God from becoming tainted: and although it purifies natural faith in God it only reaches its ultimate fulfilment in faith in Christ. The crisis of wisdom and the doubt concerning God stirred up by the agony produced by evil are not finally ended or removed except by the Incarnate Word, come himself to take to himself all the evil of the world, except sin, introducing in a mysterious way evil into the Godhead, teaching men that all wisdom is vain which rejects the Cross of the Redeemer. The suffering of faith thus becomes an image of the suffering of the God-Man. What happened on Good Friday proves that the truth about evil is

indeed to be found in the death of God. So faith can grant
that atheism is right in the same moment that it overcomes
atheism, for the Passion, death and Resurrection of Christ are
one and the same certain truth. And when faith has passed
through the fire of this agony it is invincible.

PERFECT ATHEISM AND PERFECT FAITH

Jacques Maritain asks: "Which of the two, the atheist or
the saint, is more uncompromising, more whole-hearted,
more sternly strict? Which takes the axe more deeply to the
roots of the tree? Which makes the more complete break, the
greater and more radical breach?" The reply he gives throws a
wonderful light on this argument between atheism and faith,
an argument which only the experience of the saints can properly conclude. There is at the very origin of sanctity an act of
breaking away infinitely more profound than all rebellion and
all despair: "things as they are are intolerable", so they must
not be tolerated; and to strip oneself of all things in order to
live in and for and by God is to attack evil in the only way
which does not come to terms with it, but which carries off the
victory by the power of the Cross and by the imitation of
Christ. Perfect faith, then, and it is only perfect in the saint,
supposes an attitude of non-acceptance of the world, total and
without regrets in its sublime simplicity. There is, Maritain
goes on, in this attitude "a flash of intuition and of will" which
is "above all human morality. . . . To redeem the created
world the saint makes war on all its fabric with the naked
weapons of truth and love. That war begins in the deepest
and most hidden recesses of his soul and of his desires, and will
end in the coming of a new earth and a new heaven, when all
the powers of this world will be brought low and what is now
despised will be exalted." And "God has set the example"
for this war the saint must wage by calling forth the fighting
witness of the prophets and by giving his Son "that he might
be rejected by the world and suffer and die and so redeem

the world."[4] This sanctity which breaks with the world, or, more precisely, with the evil which is in the world, is free from all Manichean sympathies; it is careful not to blaspheme against the earth, which becomes for the saint, who puts God before the earth and loves it in God, more sweetly and more poignantly beautiful; it must not be abandoned but preserved from evil and from nothingness so that in the end it may show forth more clearly the mystery of God. By reason and by grace, it is impossible for faith to lack God if it blesses existence in gladness of heart and in heroic resistance to evil: but sanctity is needed, as Maritain rightly says, and perfect faith.

Then, faith judges and is not judged. It decides among all the forms of atheism and deals justly with them in doing them justice. Atheism which is natural or political absolutism is basically only devotion to a God who is confused with the harmony of the world, with the course of history, with pagan religion, which explains and excuses evil and the enslavement of the people and the suffering of the innocent by the necessities of ordered progress. "Such a God", to quote Maritain again, "would certainly be the unique supreme Being, but changed into an idol, the Jupiter of this world, the God of achievement knowing no law, of pure fact elevated into law." In the view of such a God, the saint must be "a complete atheist, the most atheist of men precisely because he will only worship God".[5] Of such an atheism, which claims to give life to such a God, we must say that it is not atheist enough, that it is afraid to descend into the tragic depths of atheism but rather turns aside into the cowardly discretion of systems of thought which indicate the old age of the world and the servitude of man. But for that other atheism, which will have nothing to do with gods or mythologies or systems of thought which compensate for evil and console mankind, faith feels a profound understanding, especially when sanctity has made it perfect. The

[4] Jacques Maritain, *La signification de l'athéisme contemporain*, Desclée de Brouwer, 1949, pp. 22 and 29.
[5] *Op. cit.*, pp. 25, 27.

faith of the saint passes through the darkness of the senses and of the intellect, experiences the emptiness of images and the nothingness of ideas, which at first seem to represent and circumscribe God; it shares with this sort of atheist moral absolutism that grievous suffering inflicted by the world, that mixture of good and evil, of sense and meaninglessness, on the heart of man, which is humbled and made great, tested and illuminated, by the Idea of the Good it carries within itself. This faith makes its own all that the most profound atheism has discovered of the pathos of man's condition, except despair and nihilism. It knows this kind of atheism better than it knows itself. For by its recourse to a moral absolute, by its tragic rejection of the world and of evil, atheism brings down without hope of recovery all forms of materialism or positivism, it bears witness to a force in man beyond his natural powers, and, despite itself, confesses God.

Because of his knowledge of the mystery of evil, Dostoevsky had a profound understanding of the bases of atheism. No one better than he understood that evil and atheism inflicted the same suffering on faith. Because man's conscience cannot bear evil, and because God seems silent and inactive while the mystery of evil is accomplished—for example, in the despairing suicide of the child in *The Possessed*—therein is the source both of a tragic atheism and of a heroic faith: this is the final choice offered by this world to any man worthy of the name. So Bishop Tikhon could say to Stavrogin: "Perfect atheism stands on the last step but one at the top of the staircase that leads to perfect faith." Reducing pious platitudes and impious argument to nothing, that is the most profound thing ever said about atheism. The rest is silence, the wordless struggle between grace and despair.

God is dead. True indeed, if God is the great god Pan, the God of nature, the God of the flesh, the God of the State who justifies the will to power, or the ambiguous God of poetic deception. God is dead: a truth still more true if God is God made man, who died on Calvary in the deepest and darkest pit of human history so as to divide for ever good from evil. Evil is the defeat of God: the Passion of the God-Man is the defeat of evil. Every man knows that God exists; but as a pilgrim in a dark world, working at earthly tasks at once sublime and yet terrible, set on the earth to be at once conqueror and victim of the earth, man would lose the memory of what he ought to know with absolute certainty had not God himself, by living and dying as man, come to remind him that he was Being and he was Life. That atheism which admits Good Friday and denies Easter Sunday is, like all that is genuine here on earth, in God's service. May our feeble faith not refuse to face the supreme and agonizing test of this challenge: "Not without suffering does Jacob wrestle all night with the Angel: he comes out of the struggle ravaged and consecrated."[6] He comes out of it in the certitude, tested by the fire, that there is Someone.

[6] So Daniel-Rops at the inaugural meeting of the Semaine des Intellectuels catholiques, Sunday, November 8th, 1953 (*Monde moderne et sens de Dieu:* Editions Horay, p. 24).

SELECT BIBLIOGRAPHY

(An asterisk denotes works by non-Catholics)

In this series: JOLIVET, Régis: *The God of Reason*; JOLY, Eugène: *What is Faith?*; TRETHOWAN, Illtyd: *The Basis of Belief.*

*BERLIN, Isaiah: *Karl Marx*, London, Thornton Butterworth, and New York, Oxford Univ. Press, 1939.

*BONIFAZI, C.: *Christendom Attacked: A Comparison of Kierkegaard and Nietzsche*, London, Rockliff, 1953.

DANIÉLOU, Jean, S.J.: *God and Us*, London, Mowbray, 1957 (American edn, *God and the Ways of Knowing*, New York, Meridian Books, 1957).

D'ARCY, M. C., S.J.: *Belief and Reason*, London, Burns Oates, 1944, and Springfield, Ill., Templegate, 1947; *The Nature of Belief*, London and New York, Sheed and Ward, 1951.

HAWKINS, D. B. J.: *Essentials of Theism*, London, 1949, New York, 1950, Sheed and Ward.

*HEGEL, Georg Wilhelm Friedrich: *Early Theological Writings*, trans. T. M. Knox with an Introduction and Fragments trans. Richard Kroner, Chicago, Univ. of Chicago Press, 1948.

*KUHN, Helmut: *Encounter with Nothingness, An Essay on Existentialism*, London, Methuen, 1951.

LUBAC, Henri de, S.J.: *The Drama of Atheistic Humanism*, London and New York, Sheed and Ward, 1953.

MARITAIN, Jacques: *True Humanism*, trans. Margot Adamson, London, Bles, and New York, Scribners, 1938.

*MASCALL, E. L.: *He Who Is, a Study in Traditional Theism*, London and New York, Longmans, 1943.

*NIETZSCHE, Friedrich: *Complete Writings*, authorized English translation, ed. O. Levy, London, Allen and Unwin, and New York, Macmillan, 1909–13.

PASCAL, Blaise: *Pensées*, trans. and ed. W. F. Trotter, introd. T. S. Eliot, London, Dent, and New York, Dutton, 1958.

PONTIFEX, Mark: *The Existence of God*, London and New York, Sheed and Ward, 1953.

All titles are subject to change.